T0064435

Majestic Revolt

(A Play)

Majestic Revolt

(A Play)

Peter. E. Omoko

malthouse MP

Malthouse Press Limited

Lagos, Benin, Ibadan, Jos, Port-Harcourt, Zaria

© Peter E. Omoko 2016
First Published 2016
ISBN 978-978-540-704-4

Published by
Malthouse Press Limited
43 Onitana Street, Off Stadium Hotel Road,
Surulere, Lagos, Lagos State
E-mail: malthouse_press@yahoo.com
malthouselagos@gmail.com
Tel: +234 (0)802 600 3203

All rights reserved. No part of this publication may be reproduced, transmitted, transcribed, stored in a retrieval system or translated into any language or computer language, in any form or by any means, electronic, mechanical, magnetic, chemical, thermal, manual or otherwise, without the prior consent in writing of Malthouse Press Limited, Lagos, Nigeria.

This book is sold subject to the condition that it shall not by way of trade, or otherwise, be lent, re-sold, hired out, or otherwise circulated without the publisher's prior consent in writing, in any form of binding or cover other than in which it is published and without a similar condition, including this condition, being imposed on the subsequent purchaser.

Dedication

To all patriots who stood against oppression and exploitation in the land

Author's Note

In April 1927, the British colonial government introduced "head" tax (*osa uyovwin*) to the former Warri Province. On July 1927, the people of the Province revolted against the imposition of the tax. The decision for the mass uprising was taken at a joint congress of the Urhobo, Itsekiri, Ijaw and, representatives of Isoko, and Ukwuani held at Igbudu Quarters of Warri.

In this play, one witnesses how the people of the former Warri Province which was made up of the territories of the Urhobo, Isoko, Ijaw, Itsekiri and Ukwuani (now comprising Delta State, except the Aniocha, Oshimili and Ika areas) rise up against the obnoxious introduction of "head" tax to the Province by the British colonial oppressors represented by Major Walker, Deputy Inspector-General of Police in the Province. The people of the Province not minding their ethnic affiliations revolted against the imposition of the tax. How would one pay tax on one's God-given head! It is a collective revolt thought against injustice, inequality, oppression and exploitation. The people of the Province are patriots who did not open their arms to embrace enslavement in their own land. The lessons are there!

Like other popular resistance movements in Africa, such as those of the Nyabinghi 'cult' in Central Africa, messianic and millennia protest movements such as the Mahdiya in the Sudan, the epic wars of the Ashanti against British colonial ventures in Ghana, and the Mau Mau movement against the British outright stealing of land in Kenya, the masses of the Province protested and declared independence of British colonial rule. They regarded Oshue as the Head of state of the Province and he was addressed as "His Majesty" like the king of England. As Onigu Otite wrote in 1973, people would say: "Oshue is reigning and the White

Government is no more." Obaro Ikime further described Oshue as a "fiery and eloquent man who had a gift for making people listen to his point of view."

However, as it is common with popular revolts during colonial rule, the British brought armed troops to quell the revolt – though not without assistance from the indigenous people themselves. Oshue was arrested on November 9, 1927. He was tried and jailed for two years with hard labour. Many of the leaders of the revolt were also jailed. Some Urhobo and Isoko male children born at the time were named "Waka" (a corruption of the English name Walker who was the Deputy Inspector-General of Police in Warri Province during the uprising) in memory of the bitter experience.

The 1927 Anti-Tax Movement in Warri Province spread across the River Niger to Owerri Province in 1929 where women led the revolt in what is generally known as "Aba Women Riot" in colonial records.

When studied against the backdrop of contemporary Nigeria/Niger Delta politics, the 1927 revolt was a landmark in the "resource control" struggle of the oppressed, marginalized, and exploited people of the oil-rich Niger Delta.

Majestic Revolt was premiered in a slightly different version by the students of the Department of Languages and Linguistics, Delta State University, Abraka at the 81st Anniversary of the Anti-Tax Movement held at the ASCAN Hall of Delta State University, Abraka, Nigeria on July 27, 2008 with the following cast:

OSHUE OGBIYERIN	Abuke Lawrence
IMONI (Oshue's wife)	Eloho Evelyn
EDA OTUEDON	Imu Famous
BOZIMO	Tortor Dora Douye
IGHALE	Juliet Onakome
ARIHAGBORIE	Enajeroh O. Bernard
EFEREBRUDU	Ufuoma Council
ERHUEN	Loveth Commander
MAJOR WALKER	Overere Benjamin
MR. DE LA MOTHE	Nita O. Akponah
MR. LAMBERT	Eruotor Emmanuel
OTUBU	Ekiugbo Oghenesuowho
GBUDJE	Omosewerha C. Elu
OMUDJE	Omoni Evans
HUNTER	Edu Oghenetega Pleasure
1st FARMER	Offiah Eunice Unoma
2nd FARMER	Beatrice Egosivwe
SERGEANT SCOT	Oke F. Obomure
OGBARIEMU	Temisanren V. Edafe
UDUGBA	Ese Okotie
ATAKE	Tracy O. Ogagayovwe
OGUMA	Okolo-Obi Bosio
OKPODU	Ovieraye Akpoigbe
MESSENGER	Ubogu Kevwe

UKEDI	Ibikoro Trust
CHIEF AREDE	Oghenero Blessing
CHIEF FAKADEI	Ovigue Pokpeh
ELDER ZUOKOMO	Edu Oghenetega Pleasure
CAPTAIN	Eruotor Emmanuel
MR.TUNA	Oke F. Obomure
OFUOTA (The drunk.)	Ubogu Kevwe
MITINI	Macaulay Paul
BOY	Omoni Evans
PIRATES	Ibikoro Trust/Ese Okotie
UMOKA	Ovigue Pokpeh
TOWNCRIER	Offiah Eunice Unoma
CHILDREN	Eloho Evelyn/T.V. Edafe
VILLAGER	Beatrice Egosivwe
MOGHAN	Ibikoro Trust
ELDER EYITONYE	Macaulay Paul

Characters

Oshue Ogbiyerin
Imoni (Oshue's wife)
Eda Otuedon
Bozimo
Ighale
Arihagborie
EferebrudU
Erhuen
Major Walker
Mr. De La Mothe
Mr. Lambert
Otubu
Gbudje
Omudje
Hunter
1st Farmer
2nd Farmer
Sergeant Scot
Ogbariemu
Okpodu

UDUGBA
ATAKE
OGUMA
MESSENGER
UKEDI
CHIEF AREDE
CHIEF FAKADEI
ELDER ZUOKOMO
CAPTAIN
MR.TUNA
OFUOTA (The drunk)
MITINI
BOY
PIRATE
TOWN CRIER
CHILDREN
VILLAGER
ELDER EYITONYE
MOGHAN

Happening One

Dawn. Light falls on stage to reveal Atake in apprehensive mood. The set comprises a table, a cupboard, two arm chairs and a bench. A palm nut harvesting rope is hung to the mud wall. The atmosphere shows that all is not well.

Atake: These women will not send me an early errand to my ancestors. Never! Is it a crime for a man to get his wives pregnant? It is their own head that they will put in trouble, not mine. My ancestors, where have I wronged you? Answer me. I participate in all the community rituals, eat only from the labours of my hands; I have not slept with any woman in your sacred forest.

(Raises his hands to the sky.)

Look, my hands are clean… Yet, my wives have sworn to disgrace me in this community.

(Moves briskly from one end of the room to the other. Fans himself with his hands, sits down. Oguma enters.)

Oguma: Is there a living soul in this house? Where has my friend gone to? Atake…

(Throws the curtain wide open to allow light to enter the house. Sees Atake in one of the arm chairs.)

Oh, you are here!

Atake: Won't you enter to be sure there was nobody in the house before you open your big mouth to announce your coming?

Oguma: O, I am sorry my friend.

(Looks at him with keen interest.)

Who has stolen your joy from you this morning? Tell me my friend, I promise I shall take away the peace of that man, even if it is those foreigners.

Atake: My wives. My wives…! They want to kill me.

Oguma: God forbid!

Atake: True! They have sworn to kill me.

Oguma: Our ancestors will not let them. What do they say your crime is?

Atake: Nothing. Just mere hatred.

Oguma: *(Recoils.)* Hatred?

Atake: Yes, hatred. Two of my wives, Shalomi and Oghenemine gave birth to three hefty boys last night. Only one night, three boys. Shalomi two, Mine one. They want to kill me. Tell me, my friend, is that not wickedness?

Oguma: *(Taken aback.)* Wickedness? Is that not a thing of joy? Are you afraid you won't be able to feed them? Sorry, maybe I do not get you.

Atake: Oh, Oguma you are part of the ploy to destroy me in this community. I know it. Don't just deny it. Too many hidden fables in this beautiful carapace called face. Every one...

Oguma: Stop it! If I have offended you by my countenance, I am sorry. But do not bring me to a dance duel, the dance-steps of which I have never been tutored.

Atake: The iguana can not deny knowledge of the whereabouts of the crocodile's eggs.

Oguma: Grave accusations, I shall require you to prove them.

Atake: If you are my friend, then why support a ploy to destroy me?

Oguma: Atake, what is wrong in your wives giving birth to three male children? Does it not show that the ancestors have accepted your sacrifices? With the boys, your palm oil business will blossom. In the evening of your days when your strength begins to fail you, is it not your male children that you'll transfer your trade to? Besides, they are your wives... are you not the one who made them pregnant? Or are you implying....

Atake: *(Swallows hard.)* Look Oguma, everything is wrong. I have five boys already. The trouble of that is almost tearing me apart right now, now three additional ones. Is this not death, my friend?

Oguma: How? Has our land lacked the food to feed us all?

Atake: The oyibo man. Oguma, the oyibo man!

Oguma: What has the oyibo man got to do with a man having eight energetic male children? *(Chuckles.)* I am afraid, I can't make a meaning out of what you're saying, my friend.

Atake: I can see you have not heard that the oyibo man's chief has announced that henceforth all adult males in the province will pay taxes on their heads. Three pence on my head and that of each of my eight male children! My ancestors, how have I offended you?

Oguma: *(Surprised.)* Where did you get the news from?

Atake: It was my sister's husband, the palm oil merchant who trades with the Itsekiris along the Ethiope river that told me. It is clear that the oyibo man did not only come to stay in our land, he wants to possess it and also force us to live by his dictates.

Oguma: *(Thinks.)* Are you sure of what you are saying?

Atake: Very sure. Now you can feel my pains. At these critical times, female children would be more beneficial. The bride's wealth for instance…

Oguma: *(Recoils.)* The fear of head tax cannot stop us from sleeping with our wives. Didn't we pay the bride price to their parents? Nobody paid for me.

(Emphasizes.) I married them with my hard-earned money. *(Thinks.)* Atake…!

Atake: Yes.

Oguma: Do you know the oyibo man is very insulting?

Atake: Yes… but I don't understand your logic.

Oguma: How can he come to our land and demand taxes on

our heads?

Atake: To think that this is the same foreigner who wrote series of letters to our elders, begging to be friends with us is a thing that beats my imagination. He has suddenly turned into a cunning mouse. It comes to the house uninvited, does not contribute in the payment of rents, yet it stealthily eats the house owner's legs when he is asleep. The oyibo man indeed plays a game of draughts with our collective psyche and today all of us have become his victims, tossed here and there.

Oguma: *(In anger.)* Me, Oguma, pay tax on my head... to a stranger. God forbid!

Atake: What do we do then? Can...can ...we resist the oyibo man? What he did to Chief Nana at Ebrohimi is still fresh in our memory. The fellow, despite his huge stock of ammunition, was defeated by the superior war strength of those pale looking vultures. He was captured and taken to Lagos after they destroyed his empire.

Oguma: We all fought by Nana. His mother, Omamese, was our sister at Ekpan and so the brave warriors of Effurun took up their guns to fight for their sister's son. Those vultures were almost defeated until the rat from within went to show the strangers the hole that led to the store house. That was how Admiral Bedford, the cunning beetle was able to find his way into Ebrohimi. The night before Chief Nana's empire was destroyed, our fortress at Ekpan was burnt down by the hawks to distract us. That was the tactics the house rat whispered to them. It worked...! We returned to protect our home front only to hear the sad news that Ebrohimi, that protected fortress, had been razed to the ground. *(Shakes his head.)* The betrayal of a brother truly hurts....

Atake: Today the rat is in the good books of the vultures, trading away the future of our children. He now prides himself around as the paramount head of the Itsekiri. Oguma, something must be done to clip the wings of this enemy within.

Oguma: A stone cast at him is a stone cast at the oyibo man's chief. Besides, his Itsekiri brothers will think it is an ethnic hatred. We cannot afford to lose track on our collective struggle.

Atake: His people also hold some grudges against him. He has denied the children of their late Olu to have access to their father's properties and throne…If he is captured, then the oyibo man can be fought from all fronts.

Oguma: His kind are everywhere, even in this community. Elders who can sell their children for only a morsel.

Atake: *(Recoils.)* My friend, we are doomed. The antelope escapes from the hunter's trap and before it could relish its good fortune, it is hit by the hunter's bullet.

Oguma: What a dilemma!

Atake: I'm afraid, that is the situation we are in right now.

Oguma: Osonobruwhe, hear the supplications of your children.

Atake: The vultures have their spies around. Any rabbit that tries to be smart will be smoked out of hiding. A dilemma… a dilemma…

Oguma: I wonder the evil tide that brought them to our land. Where did we fail in our sacrifices to the gods? Like the stubborn water hyacinth, they have come to possess our shores, refusing to give us space even to wash our faces in our own rivers. Every day the oyibo man this, the oyibo man that. Who knows, he can walk up to our homes and tell us when to sleep with our wives.

Atake: God forbid. Does he understand our culture?

Oguma: He doesn't need to. What he needs are his guns and the so-called native courts. His rats, our fellow brothers, will always be there to place a huge fine on your head.

Atake: Funny enough our brothers are there making sure that his decisions are carried out to the letter. Brother assisting a cursed race to oppress their fellow brothers. The ancestors will strike them with strange ailments.

Oguma: *Ise*! Atake, do you know the vultures have started teaching us how to marry?

Atake: In our land? What does he know about our culture? Who appoints him a teacher over us?

Oguma: That is what they do in their church in Warri. They said the priest told them that before a man can meet their God in heaven, he must marry only one wife. Ogurubo was asked to divorce three of his wives and remain with only one in order to go to heaven to meet God.

Atake: Suits him well. Was he not the one who went there on his own volition?

Oguma: *(Chuckles.)* He left the church angrily but not without accusing the priest of making passes at his junior wife, Tuwere.

Atake: No. He shouldn't leave. He is the cricket, always looking for the best spot to fall on. He wants to go to heaven to meet the oyibo man's God so that he can live forever and not die. Our people are very foolish o. When he goes to heaven, and the festival of ancestral worship comes, who would his children pour drinks to? That was why I told my son who plans to be an altar boy to the priest at Okurekpo to choose between the name of my ancestors and the altar.

Oguma: Is it true that as an altar boy he will not be allowed to marry and have his own children?

Atake: I don't know. All I know is that I have stopped him from dragging my name to the mud. If he disobeys, then he ceases to be my son.

Oguma: That same tide that brought them to our land uninvited should take them back to wherever they came from.

Atake: *Ise*! My problem is this head tax thing. Won't our people rise against the foreigners on this?

Oguma: Are you not part of the people? After all, the noose is already tied around your neck. What are you planning to do?

Atake: Suicide! I shall commit suicide instead of paying tax on my head to a stranger in my land. It shall be over my dead body.

Oguma: Coward…! Coward… that's what you are… If you commit suicide will it stop the vultures from preying on your children? Will it stop them? Atake, answer me.

Atake: I am so confused. It is so inevitable. The snail tries hard, yet it cannot pull off its shell.

Oguma: We must all come together to resist the hawks that try to prey on us. All of us. You, me, and the elders!

Atake: But you know I am not a warrior. Besides, who will lead the resistance?

Oguma: All of us. You, me, and the elders!

Atake: How?

Oguma: Because you don't want to run into the bush whenever you set your eyes on the oyibo man's tax collectors. Or do you…?

Atake: The food that one can consume is measured with the eyes, Oguma. Though I earnestly want the vultures and their slaves out of our land, I am afraid I don't know how. I don't think we can confront them. Our charms can tame the powers of cutlasses, spears and knives but not the oyibo man's gun. It spits death from a mile away. Its power has stunned even the best of our native doctors. *(In a prayer mode) Osonobrughwe* do not allow us your children to die in the hands of strangers!

Oguma: It is the customers and traders that make up the market, Atake. All of us are involved in this. If we sit back and fold our arms while strangers from across the ocean come to our land to put pepper in our eyes, our children will grow up someday to ask us questions. Let me tell you, history does not remember those who sit at home to father children while the drum beats of war rage in their backyards. It is those who fight battles, those who resist oppression, that are remembered – not cowards.

Atake: But our customs are arm-twisting.

Oguma: How?

Atake: If we follow the call of these war drums… should… should something happen to us… our wives… they will be inherited by those who never knew how we struggled to pay their bride's wealth.

Oguma: *(Chuckles.)* You amaze me, Atake. We are talking of heads here and you are speaking of caps. Is it only in wars that people die?

Atake: Forgive me. Am…am…

Oguma: If we must stand with our heads on our neck, with our dignity as a people intact, we must all stand against this unjust policy of those foreign vultures.

(The "gum", "gum", "gum" of the Towncrier's bell hits the stage. First, mildly, then increases until he becomes visible. Passers-by stand at intervals to listen to the announcement. Children play and dance around him as he makes his announcement across the village.)

Towncrier: People of our dear land. Brave male children of our land. Open your ears wide that you may hear clearly the words coming out of my mouth. The day after tomorrow, I repeat, the day after tomorrow, all of us - you, me, and the elders - all of us must attend the congress of the people of the land, the people of the province at Igbudu Town Hall. Fathers, mothers, youths...all of us must attend. I have made my announcements to listening ears...

(Town crier moves to another corner of the stage, starting his proclamation all over again into the winds.)

Oguma: Can you hear that? I told you, our people are not cowards. They will not allow a stranger to put pepper in our eyes and at the same time bar us from going to the river to wash our eyes. I shall be there...I shall be there... *(Exits.)*

Atake: *(Thinks.)* Wait for me! Oguma, wait for me! *(Exits.)*

(Light fades out.)

Happening Two

The scene is the Community Town Hall at Igbudu in Warri. Day, July 17, 1927. Light falls on stage to reveal the hall already seated by elders and youths. The stage is arranged in a way that the main entrance to the hall is visible to the high table. Elders can be seen seated according to their clans which they represent facing the high table, each differentiated by his attire. Able- bodied youths are either sitting or standing behind the elders, while women and children are standing by the windows trying to catch a glimpse of what is happening in the hall.

The atmosphere in the hall is a bit tense as voices can be heard from every corner of the hall. Oshue enters, dressed in an Urhobo traditional attire. He sits on the high table and consults with Eda Otuedon who displays a letter supposed to have come from Herbert Macaulay, the leader of the Democratic Party in Lagos. He clears his throat and tries to address the people who by now have become so engrossed in their arguments.

Oshue: My people, please calm down. I hope you did not come here just to argue and then retire to your various homes, thinking that your problems are solved. (*Still not getting the required attention)*

Drunk: No. It is only a madman... In fact a drunk that goes to sleep with his roof on fire.

Gbudje: Wait o! Please listen. Can't you see our leader is on his feet, talking?

Otubu: These women, please shut your big mouths!

(Some calmness is restored)

Oshue: (*Stands*) Elders of our Province, I greet you all!

All: We greet you also...!

Oshue: It gives me great joy to see you all present today in this congress despite the short notice. It shows that the people of our Province can still act as one. It is with a heart full of joy that I welcome you all.

(Pauses) That the oyibo man has planned to impose the payment of head- tax on us is no longer news.
(Looks round)
Leaders of our great Province, we called this congress today to inform you that the foreigners are no longer satisfied with the reception we have given to them. But I must tell you this, it will not be acceptable in any part of the Province that the oyibo man from his far away country should come here to impose taxes on us.

Drunk: *(Fondling with a bottle of gin)* Listen… Oh listen. I have a contribution. Let me make my contribution.
(Gets no attention, then to himself)
The oyibo man should be told to pack and go. That is my humble submission. *Okpotolo!*
(Goes out of the hall)

Oshue: We are going to tell them that before they came, our land was not devoid of law and order, neither did we lack administrative manpower. Their imposition of taxes on us is a moral threat to our autonomy. I do hope that at the end of this congress, we shall all see reason why we must say 'no!' to the foreigners. Once again, I welcome you all.
(Applause)

Bozimo: *(Stands)* Let me first of all thank all of you present before thanking Oshue for that great speech. You are really a great leader. My father once warned me of the oyibo man, but as a young child I didn't heed his warning. He told me that the oyibo man is always close to mischief in all his actions. I think it is clear to me now what he meant by that. Our people say that when a stranger comes to you to ask for a piece of land, you give him. If he returns again to ask for seeds with which to plant it, you should refuse him before he comes back to ask you to harvest his crops for him. The white man is a very cunning creature; the moment you grant him a request, you give him the opportunity to ask for more, more and even more until you become his slave. But I assure you this, my brothers and I here present will see to it that nobody in Ijaw territory pays such a tax.

Drunk: *(Running into the hall with his hands raised)*
Let me contribute. I have a contribution to make.

Ighale: What is it you want to say this time, Ofuota the drunk?

Drunk: *(Gulps some gin and staggers to the front)*
The oyibo man can make you all his slaves but he cannot make me. He just can't make me.

Ighale: Thank you Ofuota. (*Stands and looks round)*
Let me first of all pay tribute to Oshue Ogbiyerin for calling this congress. You are very correct Elder Bozimo… Our people say that a man who allows a slave a handshake should be prepared for an embrace next time. That is what we are all experiencing today. Just look at how they first came to us. They came with their Bible and some trade with our brothers in the rivers. Later, they asked for land to build their churches and then a place to build for their chief. We thought it would all end there. But did it?

All: Nooo!

Ighale: As soon as they settled, they started making laws for us. Trying our cases in their courts and not in our market squares. And the worst of all, calling our ways primitive. We have all become slaves to their laws. Yet they are not satisfied. They now want us to pay taxes on our heads – *(Spits into the air*) It'll be over our dead bodies.

(*Applause and murmuring in hall*)

Otuedon: (*Confides in Oshue who then gestures him to speak.*

Stands) My brothers from the various Urhobo clans here present, representatives of Ijaw, Isoko and Ukwuani communities here present, my fellow brothers in Itsekiri, I greet you all.

All: We greet you also …

Otuedon: (*Clears his throat.*) The struggle to free ourselves from the oppressive and criminal policies of the oyibo man, is not new to our people. Our Nembe brothers rose up against them and the Royal Niger Company in Akassa. Nana, our brother and king Ovoramwen of the great Benin kingdom fought against those pale vultures, so must we resist and fight them with the last drop of our blood…

(Elders nod in agreement.)

He displays a letter.

This is a letter from our leader and father, Herbert Macaulay, the leader of the Democratic Party in Lagos, which he sent to us, urging us to resist any form of taxation...

(*Reads and then continues with his speech)*

I have succeeded in winning over the bulk of my Itsekiri brothers whom you can see seated among you today.

(They all stand for recognition. Pauses and then continues.)

It is unfortunate and regrettable to note that one of our sons and fathers, Chief Dore Numa has given his blessing to the native revenue ordinance. *(In a renewed vigour)*

But let me tell you this: we stand here today, in one spirit, for a just cause … My people and I to resist any form of taxation.

(These last words are received with an uproar)

Oshue: (*Again tries to calm the people as one elder consults* *with the other).*

I thank you all for the spirit of solidarity you have shown towards the land of our ancestors. I do believe that our ancestors, no matter where they are, will be proud of this day. I also believe, you have all listened to the content of the letter from our great leader, Herbert Macaulay,which was read to your hearing by my friend, our own brother, Eda Otuedon...

(Another round of uproar)

... Counseling...counseling us to use all our strength, and even our blood to oppose any form of direct taxation. I mean oppression.

(Murmuring in the hall, the chiefs nod their heads in agreement. Continues.)

How is it possible for us to pay taxes on our heads to somebody, a mere mortal? Who is that person that is qualified to collect head-tax from me?

(Pointing to the audience),

From you, you, you and you? Is that person the owner of our heads?

All: Nooo....

Otubu: We shall pay no such tax to anybody.

Gbudje: No. We will not pay anything called tax to anyone. Who is he that has that power to collect taxes on our heads? …He should first of all show us receipt of taxes collected from our ancestors.

All: Yes. He should show us…!

Oshue: Yes... you are all correct. We shall pay no such tax to anybody. But let me ask you this. By what means should we embark on this resistance?

(Another round of murmuring and consultation among elders)

I do not ask you to argue over nothing. I only asked a

simple question and anyone who knows best should answer me. The oyibo man is our common enemy, by what means do you suppose we embark on this resistance?

Drunk: *(Jumps up from a slumber)*

I know the answer. Let me speak. Let me speak.

(Too weak to stand up. Then to himself)

Fight! We'll fight all of them. I say fight.

Gbudje: We should just tell them we'll not pay - Period! Period!

Omudje: (*Tauntingly*). And if they force it on us?

Gbudje: Then we shall resist them. Or are we now cowards that we cannot resist them?

Omudje: (*Not convinced)* They have all the guns, all the powers and we can easily be arrested and convicted, and even fined huge sums of money. I do not think complete resistance should be the best solution for now... There could be other ways of resolving this.

(Murmuring in the hall).

Drunk: (*Slumbering)*

I know they won't fight. Cowards...! They are all bloody cowards. They have family and wealth they don't want to lose. But for me!

(Smiles)

I can fight. I have nothing to lose. A barren woman does not suffer child bereavement.

Otubu: What other means...? What other means are you talking about? Coward! I can see that you are no longer the son of your father, the great Akpakpasimagha. (*Bows his head)*. May his soul rest with our ancestors. You have suddenly become a dissident, and like the *Owhobi* dog, you have hidden your tail under your legs...Maybe, expecting some pampers from the oyibo man, your master.

Omudje: *(Aggressively).*
Watch your tongue. I said you should watch your tongue. Or I would have you explain that insult.

Otubu: (*Standing almost immediately)*
Who are you to have me explain my words? If not for the position your father held in the community before he died who would have allowed you to sit and speak on matters of this magnitude? You son of an Iguana!

Gbudje: We did not all leave our homes and farms only to come here totrade words.

Otubu: (*Still standing. Faces Omudje.)*
Let me tell you, I know when your mother was running around this village, naked...

Gbudje: We are wasting time...Wasting valuable time, my comrades. The goat says it must get to its destination within its limited time, that is why it urinates while walking.

Oshue: (*Calms the situation)* I wonder why elders who should be using their heads and strength in protecting the future of their children are still not tired of sleeping in the arms of their wives.

Drunk: *(Claps)* Tell them! Cowards…! That's what they are. Cowards!

Oshue: *(Changes countenance)*
Have you ever asked yourselves why we have become so important in the eyes of the foreigners? Why they have remained so resolute in monitoring our activities – making laws for us?

(Elders in changed countenances, consult among themselves trying to understand the lines of the questions.)

Otubu: Ask them! *(Tries to get the attention of Omudje).*

Gbudje: It is because of our simplicity.

Oshue: It can't be! It is because of our oil palms. The oyibo man is very wise. He wants to get all our oil palm produce to develop his country. What does he do? He tries as much as he can to get close to us, import his own laws to our land, fix prices for our goods and further enslave us through the imposition of head - tax.

All: *(In support)* Yes. . .

Gbudje: We will not sell any of our oil palm produce to them then...

Otubu: Even our gin we will not sell to them.

Omudje: I must tell you my people, I have no other means of survival except that which was handed over to me by my ancestors. ...Farming. Yes farming. And this I have promised myself I must hand over to my children.

Drunk: *(To himself)* Where there is nothing to lose, there is nothing to fear. So?

Gbudje: On whose side are you Chief Omudje…? Whose side are you?Now I can see you have another interest different from our general interest... Yes. If it is not so, tell me... I say tell me...

Is your farmland the most important one in this land? Or is your problem different from the one troubling us now?

Drunk: *(To himself)* I told you they won't fight. Cowards! *(Makes as if to throw up)* They are bloody cowards. Don't separate them. Allow them to fight.

Otuedon: When the eyes see, the body goes into action. Is that not so?

All: Yes…!

Oshue: Arise brothers, arise. Let's make our weak bones strong. Let's unite and drive away from our midst this strange illness that is currently plaguing us. We need everybody, young and old. Because we are all head deep in this pit of suffering. Let's link our hands in brotherly affinity for the sake of our children's future. Our people say a single finger does not pick a louse from the head. We must act together in order to confront the oyibo man with strength.

Otuedon: True talk, brother. In the spirit of oneness my brothers, let us come together to fight that which comes against us… the foreigners.

Bozimo: Elders and people of our Province, disagreement will only slow us down. It will not make us achieve the aim for which we called this congress. I propose that we reach a consensus decision that will bind all of us in this Province. The sooner we sharpen our machetes the better for us. I greet you.

Umoka: I want to thank everybody that has made contribution in this congress. You have all spoken well. I won't say much but I want to assure you that the Ndokwas are fully in support with any decision taken today against the oppressive tendencies of the white strangers in our land. I thank you.

Ukedi: We are not men who hear of battle and run to hide in our bedrooms… we have resisted stubborn kings before. The vultures are strangers in our land… I want to assure you that I and my Isoko brothers here present are fully in support of whatever decision reached here today. *Isoko wa de?*

All: Ijooo…!

Oshue: (*Stands)* Elders and people of our Province, we've deliberated enough on this matter; now is the time to act. Freedom is never given to the oppressed upon demand. It is achieved through struggle and sacrifice. *(Confides with leaders of representatives of Isoko, Ukwuani and Ijaw and then consults with Eda Otuedon who gestures him to continue).* I, Oshue Ogbiyerin, on behalf of the various clans of the Urhobos who have held several meetings with me at Otor-Udu and leaders of Isoko, Ukwuani, Ijaw and Itsekiri here present, hereby propose that hence forth, all trade with the oyibo man should be stopped –The harvesting of palm fruits is forbidden and the Native Courts shall be closed while no arrests are to be allowed anywhere throughout the Province. Anybody who flouts these laws shall receive punishment and our people should be protected from any form of intimidation from those bootlicking Warrant Chiefs.

(Dead silence runs through the hall. He looks at the crowd, surveys his loyalists. Eda Otuedon and his Itsekiri loyalists rise in support of the proposal, Bozimo and his Ijaw followers also rise. The entire hall rise in support of him and a general shout. 'Oshue', 'Oshue, 'Oshue' runs through the hall).

Drunk: *(Excited) Okpotolo*! You are my leader. The oyibo man must go.

Bozimo: We should here and now appoint leaders who will execute these laws in the various districts.

Oshue: *(Smiles and then continues)*

That we shall do right now... For the Urhobos, Ighale *(Rises up),*you shall be in charge of Okpe areas. *(Ighale bows),* Arihagborie *(Rises up),* you shall be in charge of Effurun areas. *(Arihagborie bows).* Eferebrudu *(Rises up),* you are for the Agbarho areas and Erhuen shall be for Kokori. *(Consults with Elder Bozimo.)* We shall appoint for the Ijaws, Elder Bozimo as the Headman of the Rivers. Eda Otuedon will organize his Itsekiri supporters, while our brothers from Ukwuani and Isoko will also organize themselves into a force. Any town or village that does not have any appointed leader here, the Ekpako and Ilotu should take charge. You are advised to take such measures, as you deem necessary, to carry out the laws into effect in your various districts. Our headquarters shall be at Otor-Udu.

(Elders nod in approval of the various appointments. Villagers shout in hysteria, singing songs in praise of Oshue and the elders. There is a general mood of joy as young spirited youths dance through the town in warring fashion).

-Song-

E – eni o	*O- elephant*
E - eni o	*O- elephant*
E - eni o	*O- elephant*
E - eni o	*O- elephant*
E - mo re Urhobo ke eni o	*Urhobos children are like the elephant*
Ichiyi rẹ eni bẹn e vughee	*The footprints of an elephant are easily recognisable*

E - eni o
E – eni o
Eni ke eni eni ke eni
E - eni o
E – eni o

(Song till total blackout)

Happening Three

A street outside Oshue's compound, the following day. A man, easily distinguished by his clothes as a hunter, in great speed, races towards Oshue's house. He stops amidst dust rising in the air. Oshue, surprised at the man's countenance, steps down from the veranda of his house.

Oshue: *(He looks at him and in a threatening tone he confronts him.)* Who sent you to murder me?

Hunter: (*Prostrating.)* Your Majesty... your Majesty (*Gasping for breath)* I was at the farms this morning as you directed, only to find some dissidents still harvesting their oil palms ignoring your warnings. I tried to stop them but they outnumbered me. That was why I said I should come and inform you, your Majesty.

Oshue: Right here in my district?

Hunter: Yes, your Majesty.

Oshue: Where did you say you found them?

Hunter: At the forest of Ujevwu and Egini –

Oshue: Are you sure of what you are saying?

Hunter: Yes, your Majesty. Very sure.

Oshue: *(Pauses – calling guard)* Udugba. Let's go and see with our eyes... Are you sure of what you are saying?

Hunter: I am very sure, your majesty.

(They exit.)

Happening Four

The scene is an open field. Oshue is seen standing on a platform-like log, addressing a group of farmers who by now have left their cutlasses and other farming tools on the ground, listening to him.

Oshue: (*Pauses to stare ominously at the faces around)* Why have you all left your various houses to the farm this morning, ignoring the ban on trade with the oyibo man?

(*Men come closer, vaguely apprehensive)*

1st Farmer: Let me explain.

Oshue: Explain what? To think that cowards like you... you and you...and you could be so naive to have left your homes to the farm for the purpose of harvesting your palm produce despite the stringent warnings is a thing that one could hardly imagine.

2nd Farmer: (*Looking contrite*). We are hungry – and we needed money to sustain our families.

Oshue: Yes... Yes - you are hungry... I agree with you, you are hungry. Now tell me, are there no other sources of livelihood in our land that you should continue exploiting these banned produce? Is there no other trade in this land that you can engage yourselves in except coming here to harvest your oil palms?

1st Farmer: We are sorry.

Oshue: Sorry? *(Shakes his head)*Maybe you do not know and it is high time you were told the truth about our fate in the Province. The oyibo man has a plan to build up plantations in all the major towns in the Province. And let me tell you this, when this plantation system starts, the oil you produce would become valueless. As if this is not enough, all your oil palms would be cut down and replaced by others grown on the plantation system. At that time, you will not only be helpless but will not be able to see anyone to tell that you are hungry or that you needed money to sustain your families.

All: Plantation!

Oshue: You don't even know that this Province is going to become a licensed area shortly.

All: Licensed area!

Oshue: Do you know what that means? Before you can sell your farm produce, you will be forced to pay a lot of money for permission to trade – called license. Even those of you who produce local gin in the bush will not be left out. Before you can sell it, you will have to obtain a license by the payment of a huge amount of money...paid to a stranger - in our own land.

(Changes tone)

We have to pay a license fee to an oyibo man, a complete stranger, a foreigner before we can buy and sell in our own land. I do not think if our ancestors were to be alive today they would open their eyes and allow a pin to be pierced through by a stranger.

(At this point, farmers are seen dropping their farming tools and trying to hide their faces in shame)

2nd Farmer: What do we do then?

Oshue: You all have to rise up against this stranger who is trying to introduce an obnoxious tax system into our land. In the spirit of oneness, brothers, we must all come together to fight that which comes against us...We must resist any form of taxation and oppression. We must all move together to crush oppression, brother. We shall not wait for the gods or the ancestors to fight our cause for us. Our destiny and the future of our children are in our hands.

2nd Farmer: *(Confused, stammer)*

But...they, I mean the foreigners. They have all the

guns and even the courts.

Oshue: Yes, I know. You have to organize yourselves into groups – in twos, threes, even in fours and our clans and villages must act as one and pick up arms against the oyibo man. No arrest of any kind shall be allowed in the Province and all native courts remain closed.

(Farmers in high spirit pick up their cutlasses and hoes, assume a warring mode and dance back to the village)

-song-

Dadamu o mi mun we nune -ayoro
Ore mi mun ru mi mun wo k'Oshue-ayoro
Ore mi mun ru mi mun kpe'Igbudu-ayoro
Mi muen re o-ayoro
Mi muen re o-ayoro
Abo vworo vworo kiro dibo dibo

Dragonfly I'll wrestle you today-ayoro
Anyone caught will be taken to Oshue-ayoro
Anyone caught will be taken to Igbudu-ayoro
I'm catching now-ayoro
I'm catching now-ayoro
My hands are as smooth as the banana-ayoro

(*Light fades out*)

Happening Five

Burutu Council of Elders and Pirates. Sitting prominently in this gathering are Elder Bozimo, Chief Fakadei, Chief Arede, and Elder Zuokomo. Youths and warriors from various Ijaw clans are also present. As light falls on stage, we hear the voice of Elder Bozimo addressing the people.

Bozimo: The drumbeat of uprising is raging in our Province. The people of the Province have endured the oyibo man enough. When a stranger comes to your house, you first of all give him a seat to sit down and then give him water to soothe his throat so that he can deliver his message. But when that stranger, after drinking your water, breaks your glass then he is asking for war.

All: Inyo…!

Bozimo: If the crocodile in our pond after eating our fish still salivates for the flesh of our little children, Tamara will pull off its teeth.

All: Inyo…!

Bozimo: So many tears of oppression, wailings of blood. A masquerade must dance but to a familiar tune. Are we not the owners of the swamps? Are we not the owners of the trees…the mangroves…the soil and the minerals in them? How then a stranger will come to our house, drink our water, break our glass and yet we call him a brother? The oyibo man cannot come to our land and ask us to pay taxes on our heads. Is he our mother, Tamara?

All: Ask him. No. What nonsense! Who is he?

Bozimo: The oyibo man has taken our hospitality for cowardice. Now is the time to tell him that the rivers are ours. I greet you.

Fakadei: I want to thank Elder Bozimo and Elder Zuokomo for calling this meeting. It is clear that the oyibo man's friendship is that of master, master alone. He does not have respect for any of us in this Province. The dog says I fall for you, you fall for me – that is friendship. But the oyibo man, mmm...he must throw away our laws and customs and impose on us his own way. I say that kind of friendship does not exist in our custom. I greet you.

Zuokomo: Fakadei, you have spoken well. It was Laughter that told Jaw to give it vent to laugh and amuse the world because it knows that one cannot exist alone. Our people know this. That is why when the oyibo man came and asked for our friendship, we did not hesitate to give him a hand of fellowship. Now he has turned the hawk, taking us for mere chickens. He wants us to hide, soiling our pants like chicks hiding from the claws of hawks. We are Ijaws. We are the owners of our land. A stranger can never make us tremble in our land. Never...!

All: Never!

Arede: I thank all the speakers who have spoken courageously in defence of our land. They have spoken like true sons of Ijaw land. The cobra gives birth to its kind – teeth, strength and venom. We are pirates and our neighbours can testify to that. When an Ijaw man likes a land close to the river, he grabs it, not the other way round. Not even the gun boat of those pale vultures can stop him. But my elders, permit me to express my fears. Right from the time Ebrohimi fell to the hands of the white vultures, I began to have a rethink about the strength of those predators.

Fakadei: We cannot defecate in the house for the fear of a mere warthog. We are not women. Let him come to our land to tell us to pay taxes on our heads and see the bad side of our hospitality.

Zuokomo: You are right, Fakadei. Elders and people of our land, we are not on the wrong side of justice on this matter. Tamara, our mother, is the God of justice. If we unite, we can resist this abomination that is being introduced into our land. At the congress at Igbudu we assured the people of other ethnic nationalities in the Province that our men are not cowards. We assured them that we shall fight side by side with them. Besides, who is Major Walker to ask us to pay taxes on our heads? In fact, he should come so that I can crush his head with my hands. *(Grinds his teeth.)*

Arede: If our respected elders would let me express my opinion more clearly I shall…

Zuokomo: That we should shiver because the vultures are capable of killing innocent women and children? The periwinkle says it must protect its children and defend its territory. What did it do? It grows legs….

Arede: Have you finished?

Zuokomo: I have made my point and have also spoken the minds of our people.

Arede: Thank you for speaking for all of us. Elders and people of our land, the dust has been raised in the Province. Let us not be the ones to cast the first stone. If we apply caution, we may get the oyibo man to negotiate with us. We could ask….

Bozimo: Negotiate…?

Arede: Mmm… Let me finish.

Bozimo: The Urhobos and other ethnic nationalities in the Province have started mobilizing their people against the vultures you are here saying we should negotiate with them? We should negotiate and then fold our arms and let them fight our collective battle alone. We should hide our faces in shame like lazy dogs that succumb to threat by hiding their tails under their legs? Arede, you surprise me. And when our children ask us questions in the future we would tell them that we followed the path of caution and negotiated their future with a stranger? Is that the kind of love you have for Ijaw land, Chief Arede?

Arede: Do not talk to me like that as if I have killed the only son of a widow.

I have not asked anybody not to go to war with the oyibo man. All I am saying is that an elder does not sit in the house and watch two little children fight to their death. It is hasty actions like this that make our neighbours call us men who act without proper thinking. The oyibo man has gone mad by asking us to pay taxes on our heads. Is it not mere rumours? Has he or any of his messengers come to our land to tell us that? Why not wait for him to come here and look at our faces and tell us to pay taxes on our heads to him? My brothers, let us ask ourselves in earnest. Are we really prepared for this revolt? That is all. I have spoken my conscience. I greet you.

(Murmurs in hall.)

Fakadei: It is apparent that some of us have not been fully briefed about the plans and activities of the foreign vultures in this Province. Elders and people of our land, it is the man who carries the basin of exposed pepper that you run to if he is in your front. Because you would save yourself the trouble of the wind blowing shafts of raw pepper into your eyes unnoticed. Elders and people of our land, thieves are currently on the prowl for our nation's wealth... our heads not left out. I am a merchant... my father was also a merchant. His father and his father's father were all merchants. They traded in all the creeks around us without restrictions. *(Demonstrates.)*

What manner of choice clothes do we not have in our

boxes...? The beautiful *adire* from the Ilajes, and the royal bangles from Benin were the toast of my father. With our hands, we paddled our canoes – big canoes through the creeks of the Niger Delta, until we got to the Igbos at Onitsha. The Urhobos and the Isokos fell on our wares... our wives trooped to the shore on seeing the fineries in our canoes. They are always sure of gifts from us, their husbands. But today what do we have? Strangers telling us how to trade, who to trade with, and where to trade... Do you know the most annoying aspect of it all? That we must obtain a license before we can trade in our creeks. A license from a stranger,... in our own land... *Tamara* what have our wrongs been? Ha *Olokun*! Have we not brought sacrifices to your shores?

Bozimo: *(Clears his throat.)* Elders and people of our land, we are not snails that even at death humble themselves at the foot of their captors. We are people with real blood flowing in our veins. In any of our community, when a king becomes too powerful, we exercise different forms of resistance to challenge his oppressive tendencies in order to seek social justice. Is it not true that since the arrival of the foreigners in our land, we no longer hold our heads high as true sons of Ijaw land? We have to reclaim our land and self-esteem from those vultures. We must join the planned revolt by the people of the Province. We shall struggle on until freedom is attained.

(A pirate comes in to whisper something to Elder Bozimo.)

Bozimo: Let them in.

(Eda Otuedon and two of his men enter.)

You are welcome, my friend.

Otuedon: My people and I thank you for allowing us into your meeting. We will not waste your time. We shall go straight to the point.

Bozimo: We are listening.

Otuedon: Our merchants and warriors have been headlogged with the oyibo man over fair deals in trading since last night.

Bozimo: Fair deals? You are negotiating with the foreigners?

Otuedon: No. We did not negotiate with him. Our merchant came to us that their trade with other peoples of the Niger Delta has been stopped by the foreigners. They were told to obtain a trade license from the foreigners before they could be allowed to buy and sell in the Province. The proposal didn't go down well with us so we sent our warriors to accompany them to the markets. The end result was a war of cannon fired at our people.

All: Cannon?

Otuedon: *(Nods his head.)* Yes cannon.

We had some casualties, but right now Escravos has been taken over by our men. We came here to inform you that direct confrontation with the hawks is imminent in the Province.

Bozimo: The oyibo man is truly the periwinkle that goes to a strange shore and grows legs in order to survive. Thank you for the information. We shall tell him that our mud sticks to the feet of a restless stranger.

Otuedon: We beg to take our leave so that we can attend to other matters in our territory.

Bozimo: *(Calls on two pirates.)*

Pirates: We are here...Accompany them to their boat.

(Otuedon and his men exit.)

It is clear to all now that the oyibo man is up to some mischief in our Province. We shall stop him from all activities in our territory. Elders and people of our land, have I spoken your minds?

All: Anyo…!

(Bozimo gestures on some elders to wait as light gradually fades out.)

Happening Six

Ode Itsekiri. Meeting of elders and warriors in session. The mood is pensive.

Eda Otuedon: Elders and people of our land, I greet you.

All: We greet you also.

Eda Otuedon: The bush fire that destroyed the weed, has also threatened to consume the entire community. Should we fold our arms and allow it happen?

All: No! What bush fire? How can? What is he saying?

Eda Otuedon: All I am saying is that the oyibo man has declared war on us.

Elders and people of our land, we cannot afford to stay aloof while others fight to protect our collective patrimony. The Province belongs to us all.

Moghan: You have a point there, Otuedon. But all these years that the foreigners have been patronising us, did we complain? They support our trade as the masters of the Niger Delta. Yet we are few compared to the other ethnic nationalities in the Province. What we need is not an outright revolt in support of aggrieved ethnic groups but a verbal support. A mere verbal support is enough brothers. I thank you.

Eda Otuedon: You surprise me, Moghan. Elders and people of our land, we cannot fold our arms while the oyiboman send us away from our own land. Gbubemi is dead because he and the other warriors stood up as men to defend the land of our forefathers. How can a foreigner ask us not to trade in Escravos unless we obtain a trade permit from his chief? This is unacceptable to us. We are the owners of the creeks and the waterways. Escravos belongs to our ancestors, and as such it is our land. No man, no matter his position, can take it away from us. We must not allow Gbubemi to die in vain. We should linkup hands with the other ethnic nationalities in the Province to say no! to the evil plans of those leprous creatures that are planning to send us packing from our God-given land. We must all resist slavery in our land. This is my position and those of my boys.

Elder Eyitonye: At first it was like a mere rumour. Even when I close my eyes to reflect back into the past to see if we have had it this bad in the hands of foreigners in the past, I still cannot get it. Their brothers, the Potokri, have been here so many tides ago. They were not vultures. They came with only gifts and the news of their God. (*Points.*) Look at that church over there. That is what they brought to our land.

All: Yes, it is.

Elder Eyitonye: Our Prince, Dom Domingo was taken to their land as an ambassador and returned with much wisdom. Is that not so?

All: Yes, it is so.

Elder Eyitonye: How come these ones come and say we must be slaves to them before they can breathe the air of our land? First, it was Nana Olomu they expelled from his ancestral land. They have now turned to all of us. Even those who do not trade in the creeks must pay head-tax as dues for staying at home. To a mortal! People of our land, this is too much for us to swallow. I am an old man now. But I cannot be alive to see our children reduce to slaves in their own land. Eda Otuedon, I agree with you. We must join hands with the others and reclaim our pride.

Moghan: (*Stands.*) The disagreement with the foreigners at Escravos that resulted in the death of Gbubemi is unfortunate. Such insensitive actions by the foreigners must be rejected by all. Gbubemi is one of our best warriors. (*Bows his head.*) May the ancestors accept his soul. What am I trying to say? Elders and people of our land, I do not think the oyibo man is altogether evil as some would have us believe. You can all testify to the level of patronage he has given to the Itsekiri race ever since they came to the Niger Delta. Everywhere in this Province, the Itsekiri man is highly respected. We should not throw away such patronage. Our son and brother, Chief Dore Numa, is currently the leader of the Province. He has the ears of the foreigners' chief. He says this and it stands. He says that and it stands. Elders and people of our land, we can use this uprising to our own advantage, you know! Let's just be cautious. I greet you.

Elder Eyitonye: Moghan, you cannot come here to reduce our national interest to a morsel of selfish gains. This was how you spoke when your master, Chief Dore Numa, joined forces with strangers to humiliate Nana Olomu, our son. Moghan, the scar is still fresh in our hearts. Besides, you and your Dore Numa are not descendants of the house of royalty. As Itsekiri people, we have our pride. We may have our differences, but the Urhobo and the Ijaw have always been our reliable allies. I speak today as an old man who has seen more years than any of you here. We must all join hands with them and resist this wave of uncertainty that is about to wash us away from our land. I greet you.

Moghan: Do not get me wrong, my people. There is no use blaming our background because of a senseless revolt. I may not have come from a royal house but my veins carry Itsekiri blood. I am not a slave in this land. What I am saying is that the problem in the Province is for all of us. But as a people, the interest of the Itsekiri race is of paramount importance to us than those of the Province. I still propose that we thread cautiously as far as this uprising is concerned. We should not lose focus on the population strength of the other ethnic nationalities in this struggle. We need the foreigners' support to always be at the top. (*All nod in agreement.*) I still believe that we need the support of the oyibo man. That we can only get if we continue to be in his good books. I greet you.

Eda Otuedon: That is the point, Moghan. All your concern, however plausible they seem, are selfish and not in the interest of the Itsekiri people. Tell me! If we support the oyibo man as you suggest, are our people going to be exempted from paying the said head-tax? Would we be allowed to trade in the creeks without obtaining a license from a stranger? Besides, when our warriors and tradesmen were attacked at Escravos by the foreigners, did they ask them to speak their tongue to determine whether they were Itsekiri men before they were attacked? Gbubemi is dead today by the hands of a foreigner. Is he not an Itsekiri man. Elders and people of our land, the freedom we seek is not personal. It is a collective one. If we fail to support this uprising now, however the benefit that we might get, it will certainly affect how the Itsekiri man will be perceived in future. People of our land, we are not talking about ourselves, but the future of our children. Remember, we assured the other ethnic groups that we are all standing by them. We cannot afford to draw back now.

Elder Eyitonye: Eda Otuedon, you have my blessing and those of the elders here present. Prepare your boys and join hands with the other ethnic groups to resist this slavery in our land. Our ancestors shall protect and guide you.

All: *Ise…!*

(*Light fades out as Eda Otuedon consults with the warriors.*)

Happening Seven

The scene is Elder Bozimo's house at Forcados – enter Pirate. Elder Bozimo in apprehension.

Bozimo: How did it go…?

Pirate: We've expelled the oyibo people…the whole market burning…the captain of the ship and two of his crew, seized. They are right in our custody.

Bozimo: That's good. We will make sure nobody goes to that market and trade with them.

(Enter a villager.)

Villager: *(In anger.)* Do you people know the gravity of what you've done…?

Bozimo: Be calm. There's nothing to worry about.

Villager: We are all dead…! The oyibo man's chief is coming. I'm afraid, there's trouble e!

Pirate: What do we do now…?

Bozimo: Just be calm. Let him come first…

(Enter Mr. Tuna.)

Mr. Tuna: Mr. Bozimo, you're over stepping your boundary – you're toiling with the kindness of His Majesty…

Bozimo: In our land, we decide what happens – not your king.

Mr. Tuna: You must release immediately the captain and his crew in your custody. They're His Majesty's officers.

(Bozimo gestures that the men be brought.)

Bozimo: *(To Mr. Tuna.)* Who asked them to beat up my boys?

Mr. Tuna: Ask your boys to release them.

Bozimo: *(Makes to leave.)* Beat them up!

Captain: Hey, hey stop! Not again. I don't want any more trouble… not any more.

Bozimo: Then he should answer my question.

Mr. Tuna: Your boys invaded the market, disrespected His Majesty's captain like a common savage, and you're here asking me a stupid question…?

Bozimo: You ordered that my boys be beaten up?

Mr. Tuna: Nobody disrespects the king's officer by disrupting our legitimate trade in the hinterland and go scot free. Not even you, Mr. Bozimo.

Bozimo: What courage…! You! A stranger in our land? You have a king that must not be disobeyed? In our land?

Mr. Tuna: We are all the subjects of His Majesty, King George V, the King of Great Britain…And…

Bozimo: *(In anger.) Bebe gban!* I am talking you are talking… You people think you can come to our land and tell us who to obey eh? You lie…

Mr. Tuna: This Province and all therein belong to His Majesty. Anyone who disobeys his royal orders will be punished by the law. Be warned, Mr. Bozimo.

Bozimo: An order that my people should pay taxes on their heads?

Mr. Tuna: Yes. It is for the smooth running of the Province. Besides, not my order, the king's, Mr. Bozimo.

Bozimo: You lie…! Let me tell you, my friend. Nobody in this district will pay your so-called head-tax. My people are not subject to your king but their leaders…

Mr. Tuna: You can't stop the payment of head-taxes due to his Majesty for the smooth running of the Province. Mr. Bozimo, you are a respected chief in the Province, do not put yourself against the king's order! Do not…!

Bozimo: Then try me. *(To boys.)* Release them.

Mr. Tuna: We shall come back to enforce his Majesty's orders. Nobody disobeys the crown… *(Exit with his men.)*

Bozimo: Be informed. Henceforth, trade with the Europeans is stopped. The supply of pilots to ships is forbidden. No arrest of any kind is allowed in this district. Not in this Province…! *(Light fades out)*

Happening Eight

The scene changes almost immediately to the office of Major Walker, the Deputy Inspector General of Police who receives a provincial report from an officer, who apparently is lower in rank to him. The stage is arranged in a way that a chair, a table with papers, and files scattered on it stand visible.
Major Walker is seated, listening to the officer who gives situation reports of different districts of the Province.

Officer: Sir, His Majesty's subjects in the Province are beginning to prove difficult for us to manage. They have frustrated all efforts by my mento collect taxes. Even to implement the provincial laws is now a problem to the natives that are on our payrolls. The anti-taxation movement that started in a mild way...

(Pauses)

As soon as the Native Revenue Ordinance was passed, things have taken a new dimension. The natives no longer respect our District Officers. Yesterday, the District Officer in Warri, Mr. Swayne, was mobbed at Okere and the rescue of a man convicted for obstructing assessment was attempted. This sort of violence has been followed by the freeing of native court prisoners in several places.

The District Officer in Kwale, Mr. De La Mothe was also reported mobbed at Obiaruku and his car badly damaged. The Assistant District Officer at Ughelli, Mr. Lambert, also suffered a similar fate at Ughwerun.

Walker: (*Changes sitting posture)*What about our officers in the Rivers?

Officer: The movement has also spread to the Rivers, Sir. We received a report yesterday that some groups invaded the market at Forcados and also went ahead to put an embargo on trade with Europeans, and forbade the supply of pilots to ships. The leadership of the movements has also instructed all communities to resolve disputes in their traditional, age-grade mediated village councils, neglecting our courts.

Walker: How come all these have been happening and no one told me?

Officer: . . . Sir

Walker: (*Almost immediately*)Who is spearheading this revolt?

Officer: Spearheading?

Walker: You heard me. Who is spearheading this revolt?

Officer: Well, we were reliably informed that it is one Oshue of Orhunwhorun... A man of no particular account, but eloquent and inclined to be truculent in speeches, Sir.

Walker: (*Stands*) We have to stop him... We must stop him fast before things get out of hand.

Officer: Sir, my men have tried their best but the natives among them seem to be afraid of their own people.

Walker: What would you have me do then, Officer...?

Officer: Sir, I think we should send signals to other Provinces for assistance. We need more men.

Walker: And expose our inability to control mere natives? No. No..., I don't think so. I disagree with you, Officer. We must do something fine, but not to the extent of allowing our problems to be solved by others.

Officer: Sir..., I still think that is the best option for now.

Walker: No. I said no. We cannot put our imperial esteem in jeopardy...(*Thinking*)

Invite the leaders of these people to a meeting in my office. I don't care how you do it, just bring them to my office. I need to talk to them, if possible make them an offer ... Everyman has a price. Yes, everyman has a price.

Officer: But - Sir...

Walker: (*Interrupting.) But me no buts. Just do as you're told.

Officer: Yes Sir. *(Makes to leave.)*

Walker: Officer…

Officer: (*Stands at attention*) Yes sir!

Walker: Tell the driver to prepare the car for the party tonight.

Officer: Yes sir.

Walker: What do you say the name of this rebellious native was?

Officer: Oshue Ogbeyerin, sir.

Walker: That's good. I shall remember the name. Tell that stupid Elder to meet me at the party tonight. He can't be eating our hard earned money and sit at home with his protruding stomach, doing nothing.

Officer: Yes sir.

(Exits)

Walker: *(Smiles)* Everyman has a price

(Light fades out.)

Happening Nine

Late evening. Oshue, with only a wrapper tied around his waist stands at the back of his compound, gazing into the distance. Enter his wife, Imoni. She looks towards her husband's gaze, sees nothing – walks up to him.

Imoni: What's bothering you, my husband? You've not eaten nor tasted even a drop of water all day. What's the problem, my lion? Okiodo. My warrior – the oyibo man's tormentor. Please talk to me.

(Oshue looks at her without saying a word. He gestures to her to bring a bench. Imoni rushes into the sitting room and returns with a bench. They both sit.)

Oshue: *(Pointing)* Look at that tree over there. It has been there...alone with its towering height since I was a child. My father said he also met it so.

(Pauses)

Who knows how long it has been there?

Imoni: Maybe a hundred years!

Oshue: Oh no! It must have lived longer than that, surviving so many generations.

(Pauses)

...Who knows how much longer it'll survive... alone as the craze to get timbers off our bushes lingers on.

Imoni: They can't come and cut it! That tree is sacred to us, you know it!

Oshue: Oh woman you can say that again!

There's nothing sacred in the eyes of our new friends.

Imoni: Have they marked it out for any project?

Oshue: No. Not yet! But the oyibo man can't be predicted.

A mere look on your land, he's found useful a portion. Your bush? The same thing. Your rivers...everything is found inside. You see! He can't be predicted.

Imoni: *(Pauses, not knowing what to say)* Em... em... were we not the ones who allowed them space into our communities? Soon! Very soon, they'll tell us that this community will be used for a factory. That means we have to look for an alternative land.

Oshue: That's why we have to stop them fast.
We have to stop them and send them packing. A hen that's mad will certainly eat up her eggs. But I fear. I fear for the spirit of the revolt. The dreams have not been good lately. Like the tree over there, I don't know how long we can hold on this struggle. When the paws of the leopard become blunt, it hardly climbs the tree.

Imoni: They've almost been sent packing.

Oshue: So it seems, woman. That'll only be possible if the tree can hold on for a while. When the flood overflows the bank it goes away with anything that comes its way.

Imoni: The flood notwithstanding, the small trees it shelters will always pray for its longevity.

Oshue: May the ancestors bless the words of your mouth, woman.

Imoni: They will, my husband.

(A knock at the gate distracts their conversation. Imoni makes for it, but Oshue gestures her to stop. Calls on guard. Enter Udugba)

Oshue: See who is revolting against our peace this time.

(He leaves and returns with a wiry African messenger bearing a letter.)

Oshue: *(Sternly)* Yes? Who are you? What do you want?

Messenger: *(Timidly)* I... I...brought this letter...he said I should give it to you.

Oshue: Who sent you?

Messenger: The…the oyibo man. Major… Major…Walker, sir.

Oshue: I see. Tell me its content…

(Messenger timidly reads the letter to him.)

Oshue: *(Smiles.)* Where is he?

Messenger: Who?

Oshue: Who else? Your master!

Messenger: There… office.

Oshue: Fool! Where is your master?

Messenger: *(Points)* There… there…office.

Oshue: *(Hysterical)* Go. …tell him he shall meet with the iroko himself. Go.

(Messenger hurriedly rushes out.)

Udugba, go now and summon the elders. They should be here first thing in the morning.

Udugba: *(Bows)* Immediately, Your Majesty. *(Exits)*

Oshue: *(To his wife)* Yes. This is the right time. I shall meet with him myself.

Imoni: May the ancestors protect you.

Oshue: *(Looks at the letter. Smiles.)* Major Walker wants me in his office…*(Shakes his head)* You shall surely meet me, my friend.

(Light fades out as they both stroll into the room.)

Happening Ten

Light falls on stage to reveal Major Walker, Mr. Lambert, and Mr. De La Mothe having a drink at a corner of a night party. They seem to be expecting a fourth party. Major Walker, at intervals looks at his wrist watch.

Walker: *(Light heartedly)* Those native bitches are very agile and smart! They have a heart of a lion and the agility of a cheetah. They can take you on for hours, non-stop…

Lambert: Yes…! Yes…! You're not far from the truth, Major. You won't believe it! One of them almost cut off my dick.

(General laughter)

Poor bitch…! I wonder if she has ever had such a satisfaction from her fellow native niggers!

Walker: Oh no! Those niggers are too stiff in bed. All they ever care about is to make babies of their wives.

Lambert: How I wish she'd always been there, in my bed, anytime I get home… *(Sips some beer from his glass)* That bitch! My wife… will always be there to skin me alive…!

De La Mothe: That's the price of coming to the jungle with one's family –

Walker: My wife won't dare…! Why should she be a leech on my flesh?

Lambert: You know I wouldn't have allowed her to come with me on this expedition to Africa if I had the power…

De La Mothe: What do you mean, if you had the power?

Lambert: Men, that bitch is worth millions of pounds! She inherited a fortune from her late parents – I can't afford to let that slip off my fingers, you know it.

De La Mothe: That's the more reason you mustn't have brought her here to risk her life. We are here solely for business and her Majesty's interest. Nothing else.

Lambert: She's still my wife…!

De La Mothe: Yea…! You're damn right! But tell me. If those angry mob eventually get at us…?

Walker: *(Interrupting)* Hey! Hey…! Don't talk like that, Mr. De La Mothe. Everything will be under control soon.

(To Mr. Lambert)

Don't be upset. I have two of those bitches in my bed right now. The best you can find among the natives. I shall give you one –

Lambert: That's if my wife didn't wring the soul out of me!

Walker: Don't tell me you didn't tell her you were coming for a security meeting…!

Lambert: I did. She only allowed me to leave the house when the madness in her head had not risen. Gentle men, my problem is bigger than the one troubling us now in this Province –

De La Mothe: *(Shakes his head)*

Whatever we have to do to quell this revolt should be done urgently. Even if it means our soliciting help from the Royal Niger Company, gentlemen, we shouldn't hesitate.

Walker: Gentlemen, be calm…

(Looks at his wrist watch, a little bit agitated)

He'll soon be here. Let's just be patient a little. The officer I sent to him said he promised to come. Besides, he's one of the most loyal chiefs we have on ground.

De La Mothe: Loyal…! Loyal did I just hear you say? Oh come on, Major! All of them are the same. Cowards! Yes cowards… that's what they are –

Walker: That's a hasty generalization, Mr. De La Mothe. Elder Omudje is a very reliable chief. He has been on our payroll since I assumed duty here. I must tell you, he has delivered. I can vouch for him.

Lambert: Then why is he not here? Look at your wrist watch, it's almost quarter past ten, yet he's reliable.

Walker: *(Winks his eyes at Lambert)* Lobby…! He's busy lobbying those stiff-necked, native chiefs…

Lambert: Never trust those chicken-livered, primitive – native chiefs, who can't even bring sanity into their homes with legions of wives and children let alone persuading fellow chiefs who have sworn to truncate our efforts… I mean our means of livelihood and promotion –

De La Mothe: You're very correct, Mr. Lambert. The one that used to act as a spy to me at Kokori deserted me when the mob attacked us, leaving me to the mercy of my revolver. If not for my revolver I would have been lynched to death…

Lambert: *(In great fear)* God forbid…!

De La Mothe: *(Dramatizes)* I held it like… *(Holding an imaginary gun)* "Stay back", "Don't come closer", …Man, I almost fainted!

(General laughter)

Walker: Bravery…! That's sheer bravery you put up out there. You deserve a medal for that.

Lambert: Those primitive niggers can die for anything that comes out of the mouth of their chiefs –

De La Mothe: But the reports show that the revolt is being spearheaded by one man. A high chief. What's this his name? *(Thinks)* Yes… Oshue! A man from the Sobo tribe…

Walker: That's very correct, Mr. De La Mothe. I have sent him a letter to discuss with me, alone in my office, on Friday.

Lambert: Should we arrest him there?

Walker: No. Let's see if he'll agree to our terms –

De La Mothe: I'm afraid, that man has the will and support of his people. We should tread carefully.
Walker: Support? For a native to infamously run us down?
De La Mothe: Whatever he's done, fellow countrymen, he's done for his people.
Walker: What people? ...You amaze me, Mr. De La Mothe. The province and all therein belong to His Majesty.

(*A little comic*)

... And by extension, belong to me, you and you.
Lambert: One must be honest enough to know that he fights for a cause...
Walker: Not without motives...!
Lambert: Are we barren of one?
Walker: None that'll not benefit us...
Lambert: In vaguely spelt terms?
Walker: Mr. Lambert?
Lambert: Oh, come on gentlemen!
Walker: (*Goes close to him*) Confess yourself or be accused of sabotage...
De La Mothe: Easy! Easy gentlemen...!
Walker: Were they not the ones who signed the trade treaties with us?
Lambert: No, the interpreters made them to...
De La Mothe: How do we get him to agree to our terms?
Walker: Who?
De La Mothe: Who? The rebellious native, of course...!

(Enter Elder Omudje)

Walker: *(A bit relieved)* That won't be a problem... Mr. Omudje here will answer that question.

(To Elder Omudje)

Come to me my most noble chief.

(They both embrace)

What good news have you for us, Chief Omudje? (*Pronounced Omude*) Our bowels thirst for one...

Omudje: Not too good I fear.

Walker: This rebellion your people have plagued us with has almost eaten up my heart, save for a little string of an artery that's holding it together. Oh, my heart quakes…!

Omudje: *(Tries to whisper to Major Walker)* Can I speak with you in private?

Walker: Oh no, Elder Omudje! These gentlemen here are dying to hear from you. Please soothe their hearts with good news – They are ready to increase your stake in the new plantation system when it is fully operational.

Omudje: *(Salivates)* …Give me some time! I need time…

Walker: *(Disappointed)* Time…? These gentlemen here left their various duty posts to attend this meeting, all you have to say is that you need time?

Omudje: Your message did not signify any meeting, Major.

Walker: On the contrary, Elder Omudje. What you're seeing now is a meeting… in fact, a security meeting at the instance of his Majesty, your king.

Omudje: *(Pauses)* The time I need is to persuade the others. I mean Oshue himself. I have succeeded in convincing some of the noble elders to sheathe their swords – They ask for land and access to trade…

Walker: …That we shall grant them!

Omudje: I still need time to convince all of them. They need to be assured that you people meant well for them.

Walker: *(Smiles.)* Now you're talking – If that's the time you need, you shall have it. But remember, be swift in your plans…

Omudje: Just give me two days and you shall see results.

Walker: Gentlemen, I told you he's very reliable –

De La Mothe: Whatever we have to do to quell this revolt, I repeat, should be done urgently.

Omudje: *(To Major Walker)* What about those items you

promised me?

Walker: *(Resting his left hand on his shoulder.)* Elder Omudje, come to my apartment and let's enjoy together.

(Light fades out as they all leave.)

Happening Eleven

(Oshue's house the following day. Oshue jumps up from a nightmare, sweating.)

Oshue: *Eran*! It can't happen.
Eran! No, it can't be true.

(Steps out of the bed, nervous. Paces round the bedroom and then moves to a shrine outside. He sits on a stool facing the shrine)

Owhorhu! The god of our forefathers, I greet you.
Owhorhu!
The god of our ancestors –
The war drum is throbbing.
However they may try, the wickedness of men cannot stop the good works of the gods
(Slips out a bottle of gin from a corner, pours himself a drink, drinks some of it and spits the remainder into the air, still nervous)
Spirits of our ancestors, I welcome you.
When a child is in trouble and needs help,
It is the father he runs to.
Spirit of our ancestors I have come to you for help.
(Collects a kola nut from a gourd, breaks it and throws its lobes on the floor)
Souls of ancestors who have preceded us.
Come, all of you and receive your drink.
What we have, we share with you.
(*Arranges kola nut into patterns.*)
Aha! It is clear.
A slave can never be the master of a freeborn.
That's forbidden!
If a stranger steals a royal horn he needs royal authority to blow it.

Ooowhorhu…!

(Collects a lobe of the kola nut, eats and pours some libation and then sings)

Olotu j'omo uwevwin	*Olotu sent a child on errand*
K'ono vwe unu gbeta	*Whoever reveal the secret*
Hwere kufia	*Will pay with his life*
k'ono juwe	*For he acted foolishly*

(He dances. Voices of elders are heard in the living room, enjoying a bottle of a locally brewed gin. Oshue emerges from an inner room.)

Oshue: Ha! You are all here already.

Gbudje: Yes your Majesty save for elder Omudje who we are told is on his way.

Otubu: *(Cuts in.)* We are all here your Majesty. I believe you called this Meeting for elders and not for a child whose opportunity and circumstance have raised to the status of elders.

Omudje: *(Enters, almost immediately.)* What is your problem Elder Otubu? Look! Even if my position in this Elders' Council is undeserved, you should at least allow me to enjoy it. *(Sits.)* If people called themselves elders they should be advised to behave as such.

Otubu: *(Stands.)* Mind your tongue. I say mind your tongue…If you don't I'll cut it out and feed it to the dogs. *(Sneers)* If I'd known that you'll be part of this meeting I would have remained in my house – tale bearer.

Omudje: *(Also standing.)* At least there's time. You can still return to your house and be a king there.

(Elder Otubu charges at him but elders are there in time to separate them)

Oshue: It's ok, Otubu. The problem before us is more than our individual differences. Recent happenings in the Province call for the co-operation of us all.

Otubu: You must warn him. The monkey that dances on seeing the hunter is merely dancing towards his grave – Warn him!

Omudje: You can't threaten me.

Every stage in a man's life demands its own respect. That you must show me or ....

Oshue: What has now come over you two? I thought I was doing myself good in calling my fellow elders to discuss my problems, not knowing that calling a meeting is a problem on its own.

(A general calmness prevails)

I have always believed that two heads are better than one. That was why I called this meeting.

(*Pauses*)

Major Walker has invited me to attend a meeting in his office.

All: Meeting? Why? When?

Oshue: *(Displays a letter.)*

I don't know why. But the day is Friday.

A messenger from Major Walker brought this letter inviting me to a meeting in his office on Friday.

(Passes the letter to one of the elders who in turn passes it to the next.) I have been thinking.

Maybe this is the right time to take our demands to him directly.

Gbudje: *(Pensive.)* I don't think this is the right time to attend such meetings, especially when the tension in the Province is mounting by the hour.

Otubu: There is no time like the present. Remember, it is said that the caller is wiser than the called. Who knows, he might have some useful information for us.

(Pauses.) But the problem is, have we found the reason he invited his Majesty alone to a meeting?...a meeting in his own office?

Assuming he has a different plan to capture his Majesty the way Jaja of Opobo was captured and held in a ship.

Gbudje: Only to be released when he was ripe enough to join his ancestors.

Oshue: *(Thoughtfully.)* At least there's no ship in this case. Besides, I can't be afraid to attend a meeting anywhere in a Province which we have taken charge of.

Gbudje: You never can tell, your Majesty. The cautious toad never falls in the same pit that the one in front falls into. The word is caution. Caution! Your Majesty.

Oshue: *(Persuasively)* Throw away fear, my elders. You have to take risks if you must achieve things and be successful. Remember if you delay in doing something, you may lose a good opportunity of achieving something good. Besides, we need to tell the white man to his face that we'll not pay head-tax to him or his superiors.

Omudje: *(Absent minded.)* I think what the oyibo man actually needs is for some of us to be reasonable and we shall see that he is not altogether heartless. We'll all benefit if we stop this hostility and give him a good proposal.

Otubu: *(Furious.)* Proposal...? Proposal did you say? With whom...? A man who sees nothing good in others except those cursed leprous creatures of his kind? I said it. Didn't I? When a well-bred-child starts refusing food in the house, he should be investigated. It is either he is eating other people's yam in the farm or he has found a concubine who feeds him with her parents' money outside. I have often said that

Omudje's sudden romance with the oyibo man will bring us nothing but doom in this community.

Omudje: Stop that talk, Otubu. Nobody is afraid of you anymore. You can't intimidate me with your size. *(Stands)* Are we all blind? Recent happenings in the Province have done more harm than we ever expected.

(Commotion outside)

Oshue: *(Stands.)* Who is there…?

(Enter Udugba, Ogbariemu following.)

Udugba: *(Bows)* Er… Er… A man outside desires to speak with you, 'your Majesty.

Ogbariemu: (*Panting.*) Yes, Your Highness. War…! Deaths…! Sporadic shooting…! Everywhere, people run…! Me, run. Running to save my head!

Oshue: Where? What happened…?

Ogbariemu: Police at Sapele…! *Oyibo* police is shooting all of us. Everybody at rally is running…

Gbudje: Calm down and tell us what happened.

Ogbariemu: Otuvwie is accused of obstructing trade with the oyibo man. Plenty, plenty police came and drag him to Sapele.

Oshue: Then what happened…?

Ogbariemu: Quickly, we all mobilized. Men, women, youths, with branches of trees in our hands, we all marched to Sapele to rescue our comrade, Otuvwie.

Oshue: Yes, yes go on.

Ogbariemu: Police…! Plenty of them came and *Kpoo…!* Smoke…! *Kpoo…!*

Otubu: Gun shot…?

Ogbariemu: I saw it with my two eyes. A man was shot dead… I saw him on the ground, dead.

Oshue: Dead…?

Otubu: It can't be true!

Omudje: *(Sneers.)*News from the rivers shows that all's not well either...

Otubu: Shut up...! I say shut up, Omudje...

Omudje: (*Interrupting.*) People are dying everyday in the province; our wives and children starving, all in the name of a senseless embargo on trade with the foreigners.

(*Winks his eyes at Otubu.*)

Here we are debating over a mere invitation that'll afford us the opportunity to negotiate terms that will be favourable to us and someone is here panting at me as if we're in warfare.

(Otubu throws a well calculated punch at him but it's blocked by elders who immediately disengage them)

Otubu: Don't stop me. Let me teach him some lessons...A child who lacks home training is taught in public.

Oshue: *(Stands, in a commanding tone.)* Omudje, I will not have you come here to dictate to us the pace of the revolt. Look here, we are in charge of our various communities and not the oyibo man. The oyibo man is just a mere stranger in our land and as such we can't negotiate our rights and the future of our children with him. Besides, he has no right to kill our people. He must be stopped.

Omudje: What have I said wrong now that warrants such ranting from Otubu?

Oshue: Shut up! Shut up, I say. When a goat keeps company of a dog it eats excrement. It's a pity that you have lost the courage of your father, the great Akpakpasimagha! *(Calmly)* He was the best warrior we had until he joined the ancestors in peace. *(Paces round)* The event at Sapele is just unfortunate. But you must understand that no community goes to war without suffering one form of casualty or the other. At least it has shown to the oyibo man that we are capable of so many things. The rumour that there's problem in the rivers is false. Elder Bozimo who is in charge of the rivers is my close friend. A man from the family of warriors does not solve problems by the sword. He is capable of withstanding them there with his boys. Besides, what the head does not know, the heart does not grieve about. *(Pauses.)* I will attend the meeting just to tell Major Walker that he has lost hold of the Province. I must go and tell him that before they came we were maintaining law and order in our communities. I will ask them to leave us alone. They can go to Calabar, Lagos, even Benin to collect their head taxes. This Province is ours and ours it shall remain.

Omudje: *(Calmly.)*You've all misunderstood me. My fellow elders, whoever desires the king's honour does not go against the laws of the land. I still think we have all failed to give the oyibo man a chance to tell us what he has for us.

Oshue: Who appointed you an adviser to the Elders' Council? *(Sternly.)* If you don't have anything meaningful to contribute to this matter, shut up! It is clear. A child that inherits his father's attire will never appreciate its value.

Omudje: *(Persuasive.)*As you my elders would say, a fire that burns in a hurry dies out in a hurry.

Gbudje: Shut up Omudje! I say shut up!

Oshue: When the hyena flirts with the hen, the hen becomes happy not knowing that her death has come.

Gbudje: It is only a fool that does not know the gravity of an offence.

Omudje: A blind man has nothing to do with shyness. But remember, your Majesty. He who comes home with ant infested firewood should not be surprised when the lizards visit.

(*Exits*)

Otubu: Don't listen to him, your Majesty. An elephant's head is never a load for a child.

Oshue: It's a pity.

Gbudje: The mind of the coward is his undoing. I have a suggestion to make.

Otubu: Yes?

Gbudje: I think we should all attend the meeting together. It is better that way. Our people say there's safety in numbers.

Otubu: *(Thoughtfully*) Hmm…I think you have a point there. A group feels safer and gives you more confidence. If we all agree on this step, we must take care to upset any plans hatched in that devilish heart of the oyibo man.

Oshue: (*Relaxed)* I thought so too. It goes to show that we are all reasoning in the same direction. *(Pauses*) I just pity that child. When an animal starts dancing to the face of the hunter, it's obvious that it has accepted the path of death.

(To Otubu.)

You shall send words to Ighale, Erhuen and others. Remember the day is Friday.

(Light fades out as elders settle down to drink the remainder of the local gin.)

Happening Twelve

(The scene opens at the office of Major Walker. Oshue sits on a seat provided by an officer, facing Major Walker who also sits himself more conveniently.)

Walker: *(He surveys Oshue and the elders; he closes his eyes for a while and manages to speak).*
Are you the said Oshue who stopped the people from paying taxes due to His Royal Majesty, the king of England?

Oshue: Yes - I am Oshue...You must understand this, Oshue will not pay any head-tax nor will any of my people do while I live.

Walker: (*Tries to think of a better way to approach the issue - but continues in the same mode).*
Who are you to stop the king's subjects from paying their taxes? You must be a man from a world unknown to me...A man with ten heads I suppose.

Oshue: (*Almost interrupting)* And who are you to ask my people to pay taxes on their heads?Are you their creator? Tell your so called king that Oshue will not pay any form of head-tax to you or anybody.
(In a somewhat lighter mood)
By the way, do you also pay tax on your head?

Walker: (*In a tone of anger.)*Yes I do pay tax to His Majesty, the king of England.

Oshue: What kind of men are you that pay taxes on your heads, to a mortal? Is he your creator? How great is a mere mortal that you are made to pay taxes on your head?

Walker: *(Not too pleased at the turn of the conversation)*Yes – He is the constitutional Monarch of the United Kingdom. We are all his subjects including you.

Oshue: (*Amused)* Do not make me laugh. Where on earth do men make themselves subject to a mortal and pay taxes on their heads?I can see how cowardly you people are. If it is not cowardice, how on earth would your people make themselves so demeaning to a mere mortal? It is an abomination. Tell your so-called king that Oshue will not pay head-tax to you or any mortal.

Walker: *(In anger)* Who are you to speak of His Majesty, King George V, the king of England in such a manner? Don't you know you can go to jail by defaming His Royal Majesty?

Oshue: You call him a king? A king who takes pleasure in killing harmless protesters? I can see that you are being governed by a despicable king, who probably has charmed you people to serve him.

Walker: I won't let you defame His Royal Majesty in my office. *(Calls an officer)* Sergeant Scott!

(An officer rushes in)

Officer: You called me sir.

Walker: Take these people out of my office.

Oshue: *(Standing with the others)* It is clear that you are not man enough to face me. You called us here for a meeting with you only to ask us to leave without telling us the reason for calling us. A pity!

Walker: Why I invited you? Okay... Sergeant you can go.

(Turns to Oshue)

You are Oshue. Are you not?

(No comment, Oshue merely stares fixedly at him)

Right, let me warn you. Open your ears. That is if you have any. Let it not be heard again in any part of the Province that you or your men are causing trouble to His Majesty's Officers in the lawful discharge of their duties. Because if you do,

(Rises out of his seat)

If you do, I'll come after you. No matter what it takes me, I will surely come after you.

Oshue: An idle threat coming from an albino.

(Moving towards Major Walker)

A rat whose home has been taken over by a snake does not know rest. Let me tell you in case you don't know. You have lost hold of the Province completely. Oshue now rules the Province. Go and tell your king that Oshue has taken over the Province.

(Exits)

*　　*　　*　　*

Outside the colonial building, scores of Oshue supporters are seen waiting to welcome him and elders. As soon as Oshue comes out, he is carried up so that his feet will not touch the earth. Women with branches of leaves in their hands are seen singing and dancing "Oshue is reigning and the white government is no more."

(Light fades out.)

Happening Thirteen

(A street the next day, three villagers are seen discussing recent happenings in the Province.)

Atake: Do you know that the oyibo man has promised to move out of our land?

Okpodu: *(Inquisitive)* The oyibo what…? No. Tell me.

Atake: They are afraid that our people will one day kill them all.

Okpodu: How can that happen when they are the masters? Besides, they can easily call for assistance from their colleagues from elsewhere.

Atake: That means you have not heard what has been happening in the Province since the day our leaders had that congress at Igbudu.

Oguma: How can he hear when he does not want to lose sight of his new wife?

Okpodu: Please don't listen to him. Talk to me my brother.

Atake: Last week, the District Officer at Ughelli was mobbed and his car was burnt to ashes. All his men fled as soon as they saw the mob coming from afar. I was also told that our brothers in the Rivers have killed all the foreigners there and have taken over their ships.

Okpodu: *(Amazed.)* That means we are in trouble. Don't you think so?

Oguma: What trouble? Woman in man clothing…! You have not even heard of the recent incident that took place at Olomu.

Okpodu: No. Is it concerning the oyibo man too?

Oguma: Who else are we talking about?

Okpodu: Please don't mind me.

Oguma: *(Relaxed)* His majesty, Oshue and his men drove out the oyibo man and his boys who came to collect head-tax from Olomu.

Okpodu: *En hen*! How did it happen?

Oguma: I was told that the oyibo man had come to Olomu to inform the people of the proposed payment of head-tax. But the people following the warning of our leaders, refused to heed his words. The oyibo man out of anger, ordered his boys to give all the men in the community six lashes on their backs *(Demonstrates)* like this - fia, fia, fia, six times.

Okpodu: *(Excited)* Then what happened?

Oguma: Immediately the news was told to our leader, Oshue, vian! He arrived on his bicycle – He went straight to the oyibo man and seized one of the whips from his hand and ordered his guard to give him the beating of his life. I was told the oyibo man fled leaving his bicycle behind.

Okpodu: Don't you think the oyibo man's chief will come with more men to arrest the people of that community?

Oguma: I don't think so. He would have come the following day…Besides, nobody is afraid of the whiteman anymore.

Okpodu: You said what? Please I am going. I am not tired of enjoying the company of my new wife.

(Exits)

Oguma: You can go… coward.

Atake: The Isoko people have all sharpened their machetes to await the announcement of the payment of head-tax in their districts. Two days ago, a warrant chief who forcefully seized a woman's goat because she refuses to appear in his court was beaten to stupor.

Oguma: That means the rhythm of war has been intoned in all parts of the Province. Didn't I tell you that our leaders will not let strangers to put pepper in our eyes in our own land?

Atake: You are right. How could I have got such money to give to a stranger? Mine and that of my male children…

Oguma: We must all unite to confront these white scavengers in our land.

Atake: Let's go home. I don't want to be part of it o. Let's go before strange things begin to happen on the streets.

Oguma: You are still not a man yet?

Atake: That is your opinion. Let's go.

(Both exit).

Happening Fourteen

Oshue's residence the following day. Jubilant elders embrace, exchanging pleasantries and consuming kegs of palm wine in celebration of their success at the meeting with Major Walker.

Otubu: *(Pours himself a drink.)* He got it in full this time. I am sure he'll send urgent reports to his superiors that he is no longer interested in the Province.

Ighale: That is his headache. The message from his Majesty was clear enough. They should pack and go. Besides, this is just a warning. Next time he might not be lucky to save his head.

Otubu: Hahaha! You are right. It is only a blind man who is trampled to death by an elephant. Our next action should be against those warrant chiefs who are used as stooges against their own people. This revolt must be total, removing all vestiges of colonialism and oppression from our land. We cannot be slaves in our own land.

Gbudje: Oh my fellow elders, the wind of change has started blowing across the land. I awoke this morning to see my people in Sapele trying their cases in the *ogwa* as it used to be before the vultures stepped their sore feet on our soil. My heart beams with joy. The distortion to our ways that was brought about by the coming of those leprous men will soon be a thing of the past. I can assure you. I am proud that I am part of this change. *(To Otubu.)* Let me have the gourd so that I can wet my throat with the soothing taste of palm wine.

Ighale: Has anyone sent a message to Elder Eferebrudu?

Otubu: Oh yes. The messenger said he'll soon be here.

Ighale: Now is the time for us to act fast. I know the oyibo man will not rest until he regains full control of the Province.

Gbudje: You are right. We must work hard to counter any devilish device he may be up to this time. What about his Majesty? Is he not up yet?

Otubu: He will join us soon. *(Eferebrudu enters.)*

Efe: Please pardon my lateness. I was overwhelmed by the jubilation in town. The people are full of praises for the doggedness of our delegation to Major Walker. They have even composed *udje* songs to sing the praise of his Majesty. They can now breathe the air of freedom that they once did. Fellow elders, the alienation brought about by this foreign domination of our land will soon be over. *(Oshue enters from an inner door. Elders stand to welcome him as he walks to take his seat upstage.)*

Oshue: Do relax my fellow elders. The reports from the rivers have soothed me like an evening palm wine. The Ukwuani people have also taken charge of their judicial system. We are on course. I am delighted. We should all be delighted. Where are the kegs of palm wine? Drink my fellow elders. Let's celebrate the goodwill of the ancestors.

(The celebration begins. Oshue serves himself and gestures on a guard to bring more gourds.)

Ighale: *(Sips from his gourd and speaks in a most elated and assuring tone.)* You're right, your Majesty. But while we celebrate, we must not forget the fact that the oyibo man is only a wounded lion. He'll surely fight back.

Oshue: Indeed…That's the main reason we called for this meeting. Otubu, how are the warriors doing?

Otubu: They are perfectly in good shape and in high spirit, your Majesty. As you directed, I made them to understand the enormity of the revolt. Well, the only drawback we have is that of guns. The ones we have cannot go round the boys.

Oshue: Mmm... We shall require the guns of every hunter in the land. The blacksmith should be told to direct all his energy to the production of spears and cutlasses. Besides, the boys' morale must be kept high by constant supply of food and drinks.

Ighale: Oh that will be wonderful! I propose we cast the first pebble and wait to see them cry out in pains and run to other areas where their domination and impunity can be tolerated.

Gbudje: *(Coughs comically.)* Em... I don't subscribe to immediate confrontation. The present momentum is just a step ahead. We must not be carried away by exaggerating our strength over the oyibo man's superior war power. Besides, most of our experienced warriors like your Majesty, Otubu and you, Ighale, are not as agile as they used to be twenty years ago. Many of the young warriors we are assembling now have not witnessed a war let alone seen a brother die in a battle field. We must be careful with our plans.

Oshue: You have a point there, Gbudje. I will not also subscribe to be the first to sound war drums, because I still believe if we put our house in order properly, we shall sit back and watch them get out of our land either in grace or in disgrace. And let me add that I am as strong as any young man out there. Sound the war drum and see the blood itching for war. *(General laughter.)*

Ighale: Great warriors of our land, ever since the coming of the foreigners all we have been subjected to is to sulk and obey obnoxious dictates. Now that the ancestors seem to have favoured us by putting fire in their boat conveying raffia mats, should we then fold our arms and allow them time to put out the fire before we confront them directly? We have the warriors prepared by Otubu, one of the finest warriors I have ever set my eyes on. Let's give them weapons and unleash them on those leprous creatures who think they can drink pepper the same way they drink water in our land. Your Majesty, this may be our only chance to recover fully the Province. Let's grab it.

Oshue: You are right, my friend, Ighale. But have you ever thought it over that one day everything can be restored without spilling blood?

Ighale: That's exactly my proposition. We shall go to their headquarters in Warri unnoticed, seize Major Walker and all his ammunition unnoticed. I bet you, when the news breaks out, all the District Officers will surrender to us without hurting a fly. *(A long pause runs through the hall.)*

Otubu: Well, nobody is saying that we shouldn't confront the foreigners here. But however plausible your ideas may be, we will not achieve success without the approval of other ethnic nationalities in the Province. We are not alone in this revolt. The most important thing is that, for the time being, we've taken charge of our own affairs. Fellow elders, I think we should get ourselves prepared against any eventuality from that devil of a creature! Remember, the wind has ears and mouth in this community. *(Omudje enters.)*

Omudje: *(Smiles.)* Congratulations, your Majesty! The news of your dogged encounter with Major Walker yesterday has like a sweet fragrance spread across the Province. I am particularly impressed by your show of courage. The oyibo man must be scared of you right now. *(Moves to sit on a separated arm-chair.)*

Oshue: Oh thank you my friend. I am flattered by your elevated patronage. By the way, where have you been all this while?

Omudje: *(Proudly.)* Business matters of course! Our wives and children must be well taken care of, you know. I cannot afford to be lazing about town, drinking palm wine with confirmed drunks….

Oshue: I see.

Omudje: May I ask, your Majesty. What is our strategy against the oyibo man this time?

Oshue: Strategy?

Omudje: Yes, strategy. The oyibo man is almost on his knees. Now is the time to tell him to pack and go! Or is that not what you wanted all along?

Ighale: That is exactly my suggestion not quite long. We should attack him now that the gods have shown us signs of victory.

(Oshue and Otubu exchange glances.)

Oshue: Can you tell us your plans, Omudje?

Omudje: My plans? The meeting was on when I stepped in. I suppose you have taken some decisions already. If I hear them, then I can add my contributions.

Oshue: *(Laughs aloud.)* Oh we started as you were just entering. Let's hear your idea on what should be done to the oyibo man. You are his friend. Maybe you should tell us his weakness.

Gbudje: That's very true.

Omudje: *(Stares at the faces around and then smiles.)* Well, I will first of all know the state of our ammunition and strength of our warriors. If they are not in good condition, we plan other strategies.

Oshue: Yes…? Like…

Omudje: Like resulting to the gods, fortifying ourselves against the oyibo man's guns and confronting him with our cutlasses and spears. The gods have been behind us in time past. They cannot let us down now.

Gbudje: We would be embarking on a suicide mission if will rely solely on magic. The foreigner's gun has defied the wisdom of even our best medicine men. It spits death from a distance. What about his cannons? I am afraid my fellow elders, we should still concentrate on sensitizing the people on their inalienable rights. If they understand the power and concept of freedom, nobody, not even the foreigners can break them down. Besides, the foreigners cannot kill us all and still settle down to rule our corpses.

Ighale: I like the proposition by elder Omudje if you ask me. With our numbers we can defeat the army of the oyibo man. Besides, we are taking him unawares.

Omudje: That is the point! Presently we are one victory ahead of them. I suggest our leaders, led by your Majesty should go straight to the police headquarters in Warri, capture Major Walker and seize all their ammunitions.

Otubu: You can't lead us all to our death, young man.

Ighale: Our total victory lies on our resolve to strike first. Now that the white man has not recovered from his shock, if we confront him from all angles, we shall succeed. Now is the time for us to take full charge of the Province.

Omudje: Of course! It is how the music is performed that the dancers respond.

Gbudje: What about the consequences?

Omudje: We cannot talk of consequences now. We were the ones who shouted war! in the first place. We ask for it and should not shy away from it.

Ighale: We have fought wars before! Our warriors have even defeated ogres.

Efe: I thank all of you for your meaningful suggestions

aimed at recovering our land from the preying vultures. But I want to tell you all today that our land is currently at a crossroads. Whatever decision we take today will certainly affect the way our history will be told in many years to come. I do believe that the gods have given us the control of the Province. It is in our hands to take full control of our land and chase away oppression and foreign domination. However, our walls are still too fragile right now to hold such decisions. I greet you all.

Omudje: What walls? What walls are you talking about? We have fought wars before to protect this land from intruders. Even against those we have given our daughters to in marriage. Then what walls are you talking about? Elders of our land, we cannot draw back now that it involves a total stranger.

Otubu: Your friends!

Omudje: All of us must stand in front and lead the people against the oyibo man…What did you just say? My friend…?

Otubu: Omudje, you cannot lure us to the oyibo man's den with our eyes wide open. *(Tension rises but Oshue quickly calms the situation.)*

Oshue: I thank you all for your meaningful contributions to the affairs of our fatherland. However, there are serious defensive and cultural ramifications that may likely come from direct confrontation with the foreigners without proper planning. First and foremost it will result to fighting from a single front because our arrangements now do not foreclose the preparedness of our people in the various towns and villages whose safety are also our concern. The cultural implication is quite enormous. Already some of our elders, I am sorry to say, are on the payrolls of the foreigners, which as you know is a problem within. Taking such decision here in a hurried manner may give the foreigners an edge over us. Besides, it is illogical and suicidal to capture a man as sophisticated as Major Walker in his own domain with bare hands. I cannot afford to shed the blood of my noble elders on a senseless mission of pride. We have already declared our independence of the foreigners. It is now our Province, ruled by us. Let us protect our territory and ourselves against intruders instead of gearing for war. This is my position. *(The rhythm of Egba war drum is intoned offstage.)*

Otubu: You have spoken my mind, your Majesty. The fundamental issue is that we've taken charge of our own affairs. Let's send a message to the leaders of the various ethnic nationalities and inform them on the need for us to have a unified army to protect our territory. Let the oyibo man bear his agony alone while we protect our people from any presumed opposition against our independence. I greet you all.

Omudje: Nonsense! Pure nonsense! Are we now cowards that cannot confront strangers that have come to our land to exploit and oppress us? *(Laughs widely.)* The warriors who threatened to kill the oyibo man with bare hands not long ago are now afraid of war. Chicken-hearted warriors! Negotiate, no! Fight, no! What manner of elders are you? You will hear from me… *(Exits.)*

Ighale: Well, my people and I are ready for battle any time our services are needed. You are assured *(The Egba war drum rises.)*

Oshue: I will add that we all should go back to our respective villages and work out strategies on how to protect the people from any negative action from the oyibo man. I know he must be planning some kind of evil in that his pale heart right now. We must protect the women and children. They are the future of the land. I thank you all. Also, remember the need for a united army for the Province. You should take some gulps of palm wine to keep the spirit charged for the homeward journey. *(General laughter as Oshue gestures Otubu and Gbudje to wait behind while the others exit.)* I hope you both understand the reason why I ask you to wait?

Otubu: Of course, your Majesty. We cannot afford to make a mess of our plans before that fox you called elder.

Oshue: You are correct. Now let me go straight to the point. Fellow elders, the rhythm of war is raging very close to our door step. We anticipated it anyway. But we must be careful on how we go about it.

Gbudje: That is true your Majesty. Now that the revolt has started in full, we must brace up to sustain its tempo. I suggest we beef up security in this compound and ask the warriors to go on routine patrol around the surrounding villages. This is our headquarters. We must have guards around all the time.

Otubu: I shall instruct the warriors on that. I'll advise we fortify ourselves with whatever weapons we have. The gods have never failed us. *(Noise outside.)*

Oshue: *(To guard.)* See who is against us this time.

(Enter Atake, Oguma and Omudje.)

Oguma: Your Majesty, we caught him telling some foreigners details of our strengths. They have agreed to strike right away.

Oshue: I suspected it. Omudje, you have always been the mouse within. Your time is up this time.

Oguma: What do we do to him?

Oshue: Lock him up in the forest prison. No food, no water. We shall deal with him after the war. Go. Inform the warriors to prepare for war.

Omudje: You will have nowhere to run to.

Otubu: Take him away! *(They exit.)*

Gbudje: It is clear that the war is imminent.

Otubu: Our defence is strong enough. They can't pass the warriors.

Gbudje: The other leaders must be informed. We are going to hit them from all sides. *(The Egba war drum increases its rhythm.)*

Oshue: Otubu, can our ammunition carry us through this?

Otubu: Well, I guess we are already in the middle of a battle. We shall make do with what we have. Fellow elders, we should get ourselves prepared for war.

Gbudje: *(Grabs his cutlass from the corner of his chair.)* I am battle ready my friend.

Oshue: It is me he wants. But I shall tell him that the more you chew the *ticko* meat the more it fills your mouth.

(Goes to his inner room and returns with a dane gun and a talisman. Enter Atake and Oguma, injured. The Egba war drum rises to a crescendo as sounds of gun shots are heard offstage.)

Atake: They have recued the traitor. They killed our warriors.

Oguma: His gun spits fire and death.

Otubu: *(Agitated, tightens the grip on his cutlass.)* Where are they? Let me separate their heads from their bodies.

Atake: They walk with the trees and grasses. We only see fires and deaths. A huge black demon is behind them. The oyibo man is death!

Oshue: We must go out there and kill them all!

(They go out. Light goes out sharply. Gun shots, wailings on stage. Light comes on again to reveal Oshue and his elders already surrounded by Major Walker and his men. Major

Walker is writhing in pains while some of his men are badly injured.)

Walker: Get that boy. Sergeant Scott, get that boy. Don't let him get away. Get him. He shot me with something I don't know.

(Oshue's son of about seven years is caught and his locally made bow and arrows are collected from him by Sergeant Scott.)

Oshue: You didn't come for that child but me. Let him go.
Walker: Are you coming with me or not?
Oshue: *(Looks at the elders in the police van and then to the boy)* I'll come with you. Let him go.
(The boy is released)
Walker: You are a leader of a revolution against His Majesty's interest.
Oshue: Against injustice and oppression!
Walker: What do you know about justice? What do you know about oppression?
Oshue: Rights…! Rights demanded by a people not to be deprived of their God given land and privileges.
Walker: You're the subjects of His Majesty, your rights and privileges are limited by his royal discretion. *(To an officer)* Take him away to the van. Tie his hands against the towing rod and make him walk with us to the office. Then handcuff the others and let them join the others in the back of the van.

(Walker enters the van as Oshue with both hands tied to the van trekked at the pace of the moving van with armed police men marching behind, singing.)

Walker: (*Proudly*) I told you, I'll surely come after you.

(Light fades out)

Happening Fifteen

Major Walker's office. Light comes on stage to reveal Oshue and his chiefs in handcuffs standing in front of Walker who is seated in a more relaxed manner upstage. He is flanked to his right and left by two officers with guns pointing to the rebels.

Walker: *(Steadies himself and reads out their offence from a charge sheet.)* Oshue Ogbiyerin, alias Okiodo, Erhuen Odomibi, Ighale Umuroro, Egbe Oteghe and Otugbe Amuko...,

That you on the 27th day of July, 1927, at Igbudu in the Province of Warri, in the Urhobo district did, with intent to carry out some common purpose, assemble together leaders of the Province in such a manner as to cause persons in the Province to fear on an unreasonable grounds the good intent of His Majesty, the King of England and disturb the peace and smooth implementation of His Majesty's order, thereby committed an offence punishable under section 21 of the Criminal Code, you stand charged for high treason.

Oshue: Against whom?

Walker: Against His Majesty, the King of England. Have you anything to say?

Oshue: Never in our whole life...Did we swear allegiance to him, a total stranger...

Walker: Never! It does not matter if you swore allegiance to him or not, he is your king.

Oshue: You and your king insulted us the day you initiated plans to impose head-taxes on us and to make this Province a licensed area. You insulted us the day you brought your courts to our land to change our ways. You insulted us by killing innocent and harmless people who dare to say no to oppression and imperialism. We have our ways, not the ones dictated to us by strangers.

Walker: You and your people are his Majesty's subjects – protected by the crown…

Oshue: You lie…! Protected by God and our ancestors… You cannot come from your far away land, ruled by a despicable king to impose head-taxes on me and my people. Never! Never will that happen while I live.

Walker: It is His Majesty's dues and whoever flouts it must be punished…

Oshue: It is obnoxious, wicked and an affront on the freedom of my people…

Walker: Do you confess your loyalty to His Majesty so that you can receive his royal pardon and a light punishment or refuse and then receive a full sentence?

Oshue: My elders and I cannot be part of your corrupt system of government. Nor would we subject our people to your selfish ambition. My people and I are freeborns and proud…A people whose dignity and freedom cannot be mortgaged to a total stranger. We cannot pay taxes on our heads to any mortal. Our ancestors never did. We cannot be cowed into paying either. The Province is ours. Nobody subjects a freeborn to slavery in his own land. We shall never pay such taxes.

Walker: Do you confess your loyalty to His Majesty to receive her royal pardon or refuse and then receive the full weight of the law?

Oshue: *(Surveys the faces of the elders in chain. Dead silence runs through the office).* The devil in you can declare its toughness, but Oshue won't beg for mercy.

Walker: You leave me no choice. Oshue Ogbiyerin, alias Okiodo, Erhuen Odomibi, Ighale Umuroro, Egbe Oteghe and Otugbe Amuko...for fermenting total unrest in the Province without due respect to law and order which amounts to an act of high treason under section 21 of the criminal code of the Province, and for your total disrespect and disregard for His Majesty and the Crown, you are hereby sentenced to two years imprisonment with hard labour.

Oshue: For the effacement of man's inhumanity to man we here stand trial... But let it be known this day,
For as much as my people are deprived of their dignity and freedom, For as much as people are oppressed by overnight masters, the Province will remain ungovernable for you and your thieving masters. Nobody, I say nobody, while I live will ever pay tax on his God given head. You can even kill, maim, and traumatize them, but it is impossible to kill the will of the struggle against imperialism. I assure you, my friend, even in my captivity the people will need my consent to comply with your evil laws.

Walker: Then I shall force it out of your mouth. Take them away.

(Oshue and the elders are led out of Walker's office. Light dirge plays from the background till light completely fades out.)

Happening sixteen

The village square, few weeks later. The atmosphere looks tensed.

Oguma: People of our land, I thank you all for the way you have comported yourselves since the arrest of our leaders by the foreign oppressors. Your actions have shown that you are in full support of our resolve to stand against the oppressive policies of the oyibo man. But we have seen how brothers betray brothers for a morsel of money and a little patronage from the oppressors. I wouldn't have believed it until I saw it with my own eyes. I saw the traitor, Elder Omudje, telling the foreigners, details of our weaknesses, the night our leaders were arrested. As our people would say, if not for the witch in the family who invited outsiders into the house, how would they have got access into our homes to cause havoc? Now, the oppressors are waxing stronger and stronger while our people languish in pains and agony.

All: True talk.

Oguma: But let me ask this question. From all that have happened to us, can we say we have learnt our lessons? I will leave you to search your consciences to answer that question. Let me go straight to the main reason why we are here: the punishment of that traitor, Elder Omudje and his entire family.

All: Yes…!

Oguma: We have sent Atake and some youths to bring them here, so that in line with our tradition, we can publicly punish them.

All: Yes! They should bring them now, now. I want to kill them with my hands.

Oguma: Calm down. Please calm down. We shall do to them what our custom requires of us to do to betrayers of our collective course.

All: Yes…!

Oguma: While we await their arrival, his Majesty's wife, Mrs. Imoni Ogbiyerin is here to give us news about the situation of our leaders in the oyibo man's prison in Warri.

(*Cheers from the crowd.*)

Imoni: People of our land, I bring you greetings from my husband and his warriors.

All: (*In admiration.*) We are happy to receive their greetings! How are they doing? Hope they are being treated well?

Imoni: All I can say is that they are in good condition before I left. Not after many days of torture and threat to eliminate my husband.

All: What? God forbid!

Imoni: Major Walker wanted him to publicly withdraw his support from the revolt. After his sentence, he was separated from the other elders and tortured for several days to have him rescind his stance on the revolt. But he refused. They threatened to kill him and burn down his compound, yet he did not succumb to their threats. He was put in an iron cage and thrown into the Igbogidi river. But our ancestors were with him. One Mr. Lambert, the Assistant District Officer at Ughelli, an oyibo man came to his rescue. He appealed to Major Walker to treat him like a leader of a people fighting for a just cause. After much persuasion, he accepted. That was how my husband gained the respect of the foreigners.

All: Oshue…! Oshue…! Oshue…!

Imoni: Today, he and the elders can be visited by any of us here.

All: Oshue…! Oshue…! Oshue…!
(*Enter Atake, dragging Elder Omudje and his entire family.*)

Atake: We caught the traitors as they were trying to escape.

All: Traitor…! Traitor…! Traitor…!

Oguma: Thank you Atake and your boys. We shall here and now do to them what our tradition recommends for treacherous people like them.

All: Yes…! Yes…! Yes…!

Omudje: Let us go!

All: Shut up! Traitor!

Oguma: (*To the youths.*) Take off his stinking shirt. Put those snail shells Around his neck as a symbol of treachery and flog him twenty strokes with those plantain stems.

All: Yes…!

Oguma: (*To the women.*) You shall shave his wives' hairs and make them Dance around the various market in the village. Their punishment shall be total excommunication from all activities of the community. No one is required to sell or buy from them.

All: Yes…! Traitors…! Traitors…!

Omudje: Let us go!

Oguma: Take them away, traitors. This is the price of betraying the land of your ancestors.

(Omudje and his family are led around the community in a humourous display as light dirge plays from the background till light completely fades out.)

– END –

Printed in the United States
By Bookmasters